Māori History

A Captivating Guide to the History of the Indigenous Polynesian People of New Zealand

Free Bonus from Captivating History (Available for a Limited time)

Hi History Lovers!

Now you have a chance to join our exclusive history list so you can get your first history ebook for free as well as discounts and a potential to get more history books for free! Simply visit the link below to join.

Captivatinghistory.com/ebook

Also, make sure to follow us on Facebook, Twitter and Youtube by searching for Captivating History.

Contents

Introduction

For a long time, the predominant image of the Māori was one of savage cannibals or primitive and unintelligent barbarians, people who were far beneath the Europeans. This was not much different than how most Europeans viewed other indigenous populations they met as they conquered and colonized the world. Thankfully, most people today have dismissed such depictions of native people around the globe, including the Māori of New Zealand. In the case of the indigenous New Zealanders, it was a long process spearheaded by their activists who fought hard to be recognized as equal members of society.

However, this left a blank canvas about who the Māori actually were. Unfortunately for most outsiders, there was little interest and knowledge about the indigenous people of New Zealand. That prompted a new form of a less degrading stereotype of tattooed people who enjoy intensely chanting and dancing with their tongues sticking out. This image was, in part, promulgated by the New Zealand national rugby team, the famous "All Blacks," who perform the haka ceremonial dance before their matches. Some of the more versed fans of the epic fiction genre may even link the Māori with the concept of mana, which is overwhelmingly present in books and video games. While these are certainly a part of the Māori culture, they lack any depth or understanding of their origins. Thus, they once again create a two-dimensional representation without actually digging deeper into who the Māori actually are.

This guide is an attempt to broaden the representation of the Māori people, telling their tale from the earliest times until the modern age. You'll be introduced not only to their past but also their culture and traditions. By learning about their struggle, you'll hopefully get a more detailed and in-depth idea of who the Māori are. This book will try to represent their point of view on past events and focus on their stories and voices, no matter how limited the sources may be. With any luck, along the way, some misconceptions and possible residual prejudices will also be broken. In the end, the ultimate goal is to introduce you to the story of one of the youngest autochthonous peoples and civilizations and to give a deeper and better understanding of the world we live in as a global society.

Chapter 1 – Across the Ocean to the Land of the Long White Cloud

The Māori story is unequivocally tied with the land now known as New Zealand, where their culture and civilization rose and separated itself from its Polynesian ancestry. Thus, the geography and nature of this archipelago are intertwined with the history of the Māori.

With this in mind, it is important to give a brief overview of the New Zealand archipelago. It consists of two major islands: the North Island (or *Te Ika-a-Māui*, meaning the "Fish of Māui") and the South Island (or *Te Waipounamu*, meaning the "Water of Greenstone"), as well as about seven hundred smaller ones. Combined, there are some 9,400 miles (15,100 kilometers) of coastline and an area of about 103,000 square miles (268,000 square kilometers). Their climate is mostly temperate, with median temperatures ranging between 46°F (8°C) and 61°F (16°C). The terrain is mostly mountainous and hilly, with volcanic peaks on the North Island, while the southern one has a number of fiords. Overall, with enough rain, most of the archipelago has a favorable climate for a variety of species, including humans. Yet, its geographical location makes its weather largely unpredictable, bringing sudden and intense storms and flooding as well as prolonged droughts.

Satellite image of New Zealand.

The hospitability of the land is further diminished by the fact that the islands lie on the border between Pacific and Indo-Australian tectonic plates. These plates crash into each other, creating a zone that is dotted with volcanoes and prone to earthquakes and tsunamis. Regardless, these geographical attributes didn't make New Zealand a hostile environment. It has unique flora and fauna, which are influenced by the geological ancestry of the islands. Roughly eighty million years ago, the land that was to become New Zealand separated from a supercontinent that scientists named Gondwana. This consisted of modern-day Australia, South America, Africa, India, Arabia, and Antarctica. As the New Zealand landmass slowly drifted away from the future continent of Australia, it still had a habitat similar to other regions. However, eventually, the islands became isolated enough to prevent any further migrations. Because of that, when mammals and marsupials took over from reptilian dinosaurs, the New

Zealand archipelago remained dominated by reptiles, though they were much smaller, and birds. The latter grew to become much larger than in other parts of the world.

New Zealand's isolation, which allowed for such a unique ecosystem, also meant that prehistoric humans weren't able to reach it. The islands lie roughly 1,200 miles (2,000 kilometers) southeast from the Australian mainland across the Tasman Sea, which is notorious for its unpredictable and harsh weather. Crossing it requires advanced nautical technologies and knowledge. Thus, as the newly evolved *Homo sapiens* spread across the globe, New Zealand remained uninhabited. To put it in some perspective, the Aboriginal people of Australia reached its shores some fifty thousand years ago, while human feet crossed into the Americas most likely some twenty thousand years later. Both of these migrations used the significantly lower sea levels caused by the Last Ice Age to cross to these lands. Nevertheless, the Aboriginal Australians didn't make it to New Zealand, which remained separated by the sea. The Ice Age ended roughly twenty thousand years ago, slowly detaching Australia from Eurasia and creating many smaller islands and archipelagos between them, most notably the modern-day Philippines, Indonesia, Melanesia, and Polynesia.

By 10,000 BCE, these lands were separated by the sea. For a while, these islands remained settled only by the ancestors of the Aboriginal Australians, who traveled on the land bridge by foot. However, somewhere between 4000 and 3000 BCE, a new group of maritime people emerged in Southeast Asia, more precisely Taiwan. Scholars named them Austronesian, linking them into a broader cluster named after their shared language group. From their Taiwanese homeland, they began spreading southward across the various islands and archipelagos. By around 1500 BCE, they reached as far south as the islands of Borneo and Sulawesi (present-day Indonesia). From there on, they split in two major directions. One branch went westward to other Indonesian islands, as well as toward the shores of Indochina.

Most astonishingly, by around 500 CE, they even reached Madagascar, where even today, there are ethnic groups speaking languages from the Austronesian family.

More important for our story were the Austronesians that moved eastward. Part of them sailed toward the Micronesian region, while others went to Melanesia, reaching the shores of Papua New Guinea, the Solomon Islands, and the Bismarck Archipelago. By about 900 BCE, their expansions had stopped, marking the eastern boundary of Austronesian settlements on the islands of Fiji, Samoa, and Tonga. On some of these islands, the seafaring Austronesian people mixed with preexisting human populations, but their culture became dominant. Thus, around 1500 BCE, they formed the so-called Lapita culture, which became predominant both in Micronesia and Melanesia. The most distinctive object of this civilization was geometric designs on dentate-stamped pottery. Along with pottery, this Austronesian culture also grew yams, bananas, gourds, taros, breadfruit, and sugar cane. Some of these were farmed on Asian paddy fields. Along with that, the Lapita culture domesticated animals, such as dogs, pigs, and chickens. Some of the Lapita people lived in stilt houses, and their main tools were made of stone, most notably obsidian.

Other notable distinctions of the Lapita Austronesians were their use of outrigger boats, tattoo chisels, stone and fishbone fishhooks, and harpoon points. All of these remained almost identical to later Polynesian cultures, which supports the theory that the Lapita civilization was its direct ancestor. It seems that for roughly one thousand years, the Lapita people consolidated some of the basic Polynesian cultural characteristics, like the language and religious beliefs and concepts like, for example, mana, as well as the pantheon of gods. They also formed the roots of a social system with kinship and ranks, which are today linked with the Polynesian civilization. It could also be theorized that, over time, they also improved and advanced their maritime technology and techniques. Around 700 CE, they resumed their eastward explorations, reaching the Cook Islands, Tahiti, and the rest of what is today French Polynesia. By then, the Lapita were transformed into the Polynesians, a change that is marked by the loss of their distinctive pottery.

Over the next several hundred years, the Polynesian people spread across what is today known as Polynesia, which roughly stretches from Samoa in the west to Easter Island in the east and Hawaii in the north to New Zealand in the south. This is a rather wide area that covers large chunks of open waters in the Pacific Ocean. The astonishing feat of covering such large distances and treacherous seas has made some modern scholars doubt if these Polynesian voyages were deliberate. For Western historians, it seemed inexplicable that a culture that seemed far inferior to any in Europe or around the Mediterranean Sea could travel so far, especially considering their Western contemporaries barely managed to leave their coasts. However, modern researchers have almost undoubtedly proved that the Polynesians, like their Austronesian ancestors, sailed with full intent and the knowledge of how to do so with minimal risks.

Firstly, any initial voyage was started toward the upwind from their point of departure, allowing them to return home downwind even if their expedition failed to find land. This would also allow for an easier trip back if land was found, making the planned expedition a two-way voyage from its inception. Furthermore, these initial travels were always merely exploratory. They charted possible routes for more prepared voyages that set out to colonize.

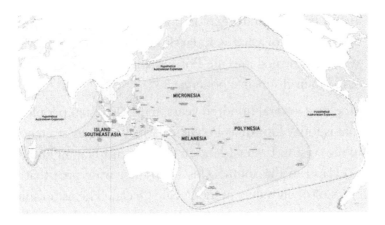

Estimated reach of Austronesian people.
Source: BlankMap-World-162E.svg: Lokal_Profilderivative work: Milenioscuro
(talk)derivative work: Obsidian Soul], CC0, via Wikimedia Commons
https://commons.wikimedia.org/wiki/File:Austronesia_with_hypothetical_greatest_expansion_extent_(Blench,_2009)_01.png

Coupled with their planning techniques were their well-crafted outrigger canoes. They sometimes used the double outrigger design. Here, it is important to note that our minds often link canoes with small vessels, like a rowboat carrying a few people. However, the Polynesians, like other branches of the Austronesian people, built large ships capable of carrying dozens of people, with the boats powered by sails and the wind. It is also worth noting that the Polynesian sailors were capable navigators. They knew how to navigate with the help of the sun and the stars, and they used various methods, like spotting birds and cloud formations, to deduce if there was land beyond the visible horizon. They would pass this information on to other navigators and make repeated voyages, further reinforcing the notion that their trips were deliberate.

If that wasn't enough to prove the maritime quality and capability of the Polynesian explorers, then there is the fact that, according to some research, they reached as far east as the western coasts of South America. There is some evidence to support such claims. The Polynesians cultivated sweet potatoes before the arrival of Europeans to the region. The sweet potato or batata, often mistakenly referred to as yams, originated in Central or South America. Thus, the

Polynesians managed to reach the American continent before Christopher Columbus. On the Cook Islands, archaeologists found traces of this vegetable as early as the 11th century CE, prompting some scholars to deduce that Polynesian trips to the Americas must predate this century. Some bolder claims date Polynesian contact with the Americas to possibly the 8th century, though there is no evidence to support these claims. Another interesting facet of this implied contact is the fact that in various Polynesian languages, sweet potato is called *kumara* (also known as *kumala* or *umala*), while Bolivian and Peruvian Quechua sometimes refer to the plants as *kumara* or *kumar*, which is strikingly similar.

Apart from the sweet potato, some genetic studies of both chicken and human remains infer possible contact. In the case of human remains, several DNA markers found on certain Polynesian remains showed some mixture with the genes of the natives on the Columbian coast. Some scholars proposed this was a result of a single contact that took place in the late 12th or early 13th century. Also, some chicken remains found on the Chilean coast were dated to the early 14th century, with some of its genes sharing similarities to the domesticated chickens raised by the Polynesians. This has led some scholars to theorize that the Polynesians brought domesticated poultry to the Americas. However, these theories are still relatively new, and there is no conclusive scholarly agreement on them. Similarly, even less conclusive are the linguistic similarities found in a few words. Nevertheless, even if the linguistic and genetic similarities are completely disregarded, the unwavering evidence in the form of the *kumara* proves that the Polynesians reached South America most likely more than once.

Considering such an impressive maritime resume, it is clear that the Polynesians were indeed more than capable of settling the remote islands of New Zealand. This is important to note, as, from the 19th century onward, many Western theories were made about the origin of the Māori. Some of the earliest mention Aryan or Israelite roots, while others tried to link them with Melanesian or South American ancestry. The former was clearly a product of 19th-century Eurocentric thinking and prejudices, while the latter was made with a lack of evidence and based more on scientific speculation. Worse than that were theories made by various pseudo-historians linking the Māori with Phoenicians, Egyptians, and even Celts. Of course, these quasi-scientific hypotheses never came close to any credible academic scrutiny and resided mostly in the imagination of their creators. Due to modern research and archaeology, it became clear that the only viable ancestry of the Māori was from the Polynesian people. Despite that, there were still many questions about how they settled the islands of the New Zealand archipelago.

The first widely accepted tale of Māori colonization came in the late 19th and early 20th centuries, and it was written by an ethnologist named Stephenson Percy Smith. It was supposedly extracted from Māori mythology, starting with the legendary Polynesian navigator Kupe discovering New Zealand. According to the myth, as Smith wrote it down, Kupe originated from Tahiti and sailed south with his wife and children around 950 CE. After days of seeing nothing but an empty horizon, his wife spotted a cloud, steering them toward the North Island. As they neared their goal, they began chanting "*Aotea! Aotea!*" or "The white cloud! The white cloud!" Battling against all odds, Kupe and his voyagers became the first humans to have set foot on New Zealand. However, they didn't colonize it; they returned home, bringing news of their discoveries to the rest of their people. However, no immediate voyages were made. Instead, over the next several decades, New Zealand was occupied by the Moriori people. According to Smith, these original colonizers of New Zealand were of Melanesian ancestry. Their race was described as weaker and less stalwart, and their exact place of origin remained unknown.

The first Polynesians and Māori who permanently settled these lands were Toi and Whatonga, a Tahitian chief and his son-in-law who got separated while traveling the seas. Toi landed in New

Zealand, settling among the Moriori. Whatonga found him there, and around 1150 CE, the two of them, along with their entourages, decided to settle in the region today known as the Bay of Plenty (or *Te Moana-a-Toi*). However, Māori colonization only truly came about in the mid-14th century with the arrival of the Great Fleet. By that time, the Polynesians from what is today French Polynesia had enough of their internal strife and struggles. They decided to seek more peaceful and prosperous lands. By then, they've heard enough stories of the bountiful land of the white cloud (*Aotearoa*). Thus, they gathered seven (in some later retellings, nine) canoes and sailed to New Zealand. Their voyage was beset with perils and adventures, but they arrived safely. Afterward, they merged with the preexisting Māori to conclusively establish dominion over the New Zealand archipelago, expulsing the Moriori farther eastward to remote isles today known as the Chatham Islands.

This story is probably the most widely known since Smith's writings even became part of New Zealand's 20th-century school curriculum. It was a tale that resonated well with both the European colonizers and the remnants of the Māori. For the latter, it brought much-needed pride in their own accomplishments, as it talked about the heroism of their forefathers. For the former, it was reminiscent of myths closer to their heritage, like, for example, Jason and the Argonauts. More importantly, it made the Western colonizers feel their feat of conquering New Zealand as a much worthier conquest due to the nobility of the native Māori.

However, after decades of research, it has been concluded that Smith's story was more or less made up. It seems that he gathered various local Māori tales and legends, along with their traditional genealogies, and combined them into a coherent myth that sounded both enticing and truthful. Despite that, it was a long process to dislodge Smith's historical concoction from the minds of both the Māori and the descendants of the European colonizers. Some of it stuck, as *Aotearoa* remains the official Māori name for New Zealand even today, despite that, historically, they never had an epithet for the entire archipelago, only separate islands.

Despite all that, there are some grains of truth behind Smith's account. For example, most historians agree that Kupe was most likely a real person; he was probably one of the earliest settlers who left enough of a trace in Māori society that the memory of him became the foundation for various myths and legends. Of course, he didn't live in the 10th century, nor was he an actual "discoverer" of New Zealand. Likewise, Toi and Whatonga were probably prominent members of some Māori tribes that lived much later than in the story. Smith most likely correctly guessed that the Māori arrived in New Zealand in waves after initial explorational voyages. Interestingly, his calculation of the timeframe of Māori colonization is remarkably accurate. By averaging and calculating various traditional genealogies, he came up with the year 1350 CE, which is roughly within a century of what the archaeological evidence suggests.

Map of Polynesian migrations with estimated chronology. Source:

Unlike Smith's myth, which seems conclusive and thrilling, the academic research on the Māori migration to New Zealand is filled with far less certainty. Firstly, there isn't a precise date when the Polynesians first discovered these lands. So far, the earliest presence of human settlement dates to the 13th century. By the early to mid-14th century, the Māori presence was significant enough to leave an impact on the local flora and fauna, as there are signs of deforestation and the decline in the population of flightless birds. However, these findings are still not seen as certain, as some scholars think new discoveries might either push the Māori settlement further in the past or provide a more precise dating. What seems certain is that before the settling began, the Polynesian seafarers visited *Aotearoa*. It is a common theme of various Māori origin myths, and there are some signs of Pacific rats or *kiore* in Māori that predate the 13th century. Additionally, that would fit with the overall pattern of Polynesian exploration and migration. However, there are no conclusive dates to pinpoint the exact moment, especially since such visiting expeditions often left no archaeological trace behind them.

New Zealand *kiore* also shed some light as to where the Māori ancestors came from. Their genetic markers show likeness with *kiore* from East Polynesian islands, more precisely the Cook and Society Islands. The ancestry of the early Māori is further attested by various tools, most notably fishhooks, adzes, and harpoon points, which share various similarities with implements from East Polynesia. Nevertheless, it seems unlikely that scholars will ever be able to pinpoint which exact island the Māori colonists came from, especially since archaeology from the East Polynesian islands confirms it was a zone of frequent interactions and strong cultural ties. Despite the inconclusive evidence, some modern historians believe West Polynesian influence might have been possible. Yet, no material evidence of this has been found so far. Thus, if some contact existed, it was brief.

Another important question for archaeologists is where the Eastern Polynesians first landed. Logic commands that it had to be on the North Island, which is something backed by various local Māori legends. Some of these traditions are linked with the North Cape, the northeastern tip of the Aupouri Peninsula, while others link it with the Coromandel Peninsula (or *Te Tara-O-Te-Ika-A-Māui*, meaning the "spine of Māui's fish") located on the western edge of the Bay of Plenty. However, most of the myths mention the Bay of Plenty, more precisely its eastern edge, as the location of their initial landfall. Archaeology is rather mute on this topic, most likely since the early Māori settlements were built on river mouths and sand dunes, which are regions prone to erosion. Furthermore, some of the sites were likely built over during European colonization. However, it is clear that the northeastern shore of the North Island was the general landing zone for the Polynesian settlers, a fact corroborated with various archaeological findings. Archaeology also indicates that the Māori quickly spread farther south, following the eastern coastline of New Zealand and reaching the modern-day region of Canterbury (*Waitaha* in Māori, named after a tribe that lives there) by the early 14th century.

It is important to note that the various local Māori origin myths mentioning different landing places may not be erroneous. Genetic examination of *kiore* has shown that the settlement of New Zealand was done in waves, meaning that different colonizing expeditions may have initially landed at different locations, though in roughly the same region. Additionally, this disproves the idea of Smith's "large fleet colonization," especially considering the Polynesians rarely traveled in flotillas. However, the names of the canoes and their captains, which are recorded in Māori legends, may be based on these various migratory voyages.

Finally, there is the question of how many Polynesians came to New Zealand in those waves. Here, the myths are too vague to be of any help. Nevertheless, modern demographers and geneticists, working with existing models and knowledge gathered from around the world, have calculated that there were somewhere between one hundred and two hundred original Māori settlers, with no less than fifty women among them. Of course, these numbers should be taken as estimates. However, it seems unlikely there were fewer than one hundred, while it could be theorized more than two hundred arrived. In any case, it is important to note that Polynesian migrations weren't as massive as some other land population movements.

The last sphere of the Māori migrations that has to be dealt with is the issue of when it stopped. Smith's theorizing that it ended abruptly after the arrival of this mythic grand fleet is, of course, faulty. Firstly, it seems that the early Māori preserved at least some contact with their Eastern Polynesian native islands. Archaeologists have found traces of settlements on the Kermadec Islands, which are some 500 to 620 miles (800 to 1,000 kilometers) northeast of the North Island. It seems to have been settled in the 14th century. The Māori name for it is *Rangitahua* or the "Stopping-off Place," which suggests it was a link between two regions. Similarly, Norfolk Island located to the northwest, between New Zealand and New Caledonia, shows traces of Māori settlement, most likely from the 14th century as well. The artifacts found here also suggest it was a trading station between the New Zealand Māori and other Polynesians, as well as Melanesians from New Caledonia. More impressive was the Māori settlement of the Auckland Islands, which lie some 290 miles (465 kilometers) south of the South Island. It was settled roughly at the same time as Norfolk or Kermadec, but its climate was much harsher since it sits in the subpolar region of Antarctica. Finally, similarities between the Māori tools and those found on the Pitcairn Islands, located about halfway between Peru to New Zealand, indicate another possible trade link. However, these islands were settled by at least the 12th century, meaning the Māori couldn't have colonized them.

Another important point of continuous Polynesian and Māori migrations is the already mentioned travel of Moriori to the Chatham

Islands, some five hundred miles (eight hundred kilometers) east of the South Island. Unlike Smith's concoction, the reality is that the Moriori are descendants of Māori who traveled to the remote isles sometime in the 15th century. Once again, research of *kiore* DNA revealed the settlers originated from New Zealand. This was further backed by various linguistic and tool similarities with the Māori. However, the Moriori settlement was among the last colonizing expeditions for both the Māori and Polynesians in general. By the late 15th and early 16th centuries, the maritime voyages from the Polynesian world started to die down. Most scholars tie this to the advent of the so-called Little Ice Age, which roughly dates between the 15th to the 18th century. The gradual temperature drop caused harsher winds and weather, which created rougher seas and more perilous maritime travel.

The end of reliable seafaring connections was crucial for the Polynesians, including the Māori. Ties between the Māori and their Polynesian brethren were cut, limiting further cultural and trade interactions. In turn, this led to the quick demise of trade-station settlements on Norfolk or Kermadec, which were dependent on the import of food. Similarly, the southern Auckland Islands were also abandoned. However, the Chatham Islands remained populated, as their lands were abundant enough to support a smaller population. Nevertheless, once they lost touch with their New Zealand homeland, their civilizational development followed a separate path from the Māori. They abandoned class divisions, agriculture, and wars, and their material culture became more simplistic. Thus, by the time the Europeans came, they were indeed separate people from their Māori ancestors, and neither the Moriori nor the Māori had any recollection of their former ties. These differences were exploited by the Westerners to create the pre-Māori settlement myth, which helped justify their colonization of New Zealand. Supposedly, the Europeans did the same thing to the Māori as the Māori did to the Moriori. These faulty theories also fit into the prevailing social Darwinism theory, as well as 19th-century racism, which saw the darker-skinned Moriori as being innately inferior to the lighter-skinned Māori, with both being far darker than the pale Europeans.

Regardless of these lost connections and their subsequent isolation, by the time of the Little Ice Age, Māori colonization was already done. They were firmly set in what we today know as New Zealand.

Chapter 2 – From an Interconnected World to Extended Isolation

The previous chapter introduced the Polynesian background of the Māori, exploring their ancestry as well as their migratory reach and cultural ties with other islands and archipelagos. However, the remaining question is how and when did the Māori become a separate culture within the Polynesian family.

To understand how the early settlers from East Polynesia transformed into the Māori, it is important to know just how vast the difference was between their new home and the various islands from whence they came. They originally hailed from much smaller islands that had tropical and sub-tropical wildlife without too many animals or forests. Minerals were also usually rather sparse, as was the available farmable land. In contrast, New Zealand was enormous. It constitutes nearly 90 percent of the entire Polynesian landmass. The second-largest archipelago is Hawaii, which covers about 5 to 6 percent of its landmass. Secondly, its geographical location also meant that the arriving Polynesian settlers came into contact with different climates for the first time in thousands of years since their Austronesian ancestors began their journey from the Asian coast. The northern regions had a warm and subtropic climate, but it transformed into a temperate climate in the central regions. The southernmost lands were colder beyond anything they could've imagined. There were also sub-alpine mountains capped with snow, which was something they did not see in the tropics.

Unsurprisingly, such lands offered much more diversity and available resources to the initial Polynesian settlers. They had plenty of land to use for horticulture, and they encountered new types of plants, which were often larger than in their original homelands. Among the large forests, which provided abundant sources of wood, they also found giant birds. On the coasts, they found seals. Animals of that size were unimaginable to their ancestors and provided ample amounts of food. Finally, since New Zealand lies in a region with several active volcanoes, they had sources of various stones and minerals, most notably obsidian.

The Polynesian settlers had to adapt to all of that. They changed their diets, and their tools began to differentiate, as did their clothing and housing. They adjusted to the demands of these new climates, as well as the higher availably of resources, both known and unknown. To achieve this adaption, the settlers had to develop new technical skills, further influencing both their material culture and society. This process of change and adjustment to the new environment transformed the initial Eastern Polynesians into the Māori.

However, it was a slow and gradual evolution. The exact moment when the inhabitants of New Zealand became the Māori is impossible to determine. However, for simplicity and understanding, most scholars and texts reference even the earliest settlers as the Māori. With that in mind, it should be pointed out once more that the Māori, despite their uniqueness, reman part of the Polynesian cultural family through various shared traits. It is also worth noting that for most of their history, the Māori actually never referred to themselves as such. The word itself meant "ordinary," and no further determination existed. For most of their existence, they knew each other, and there was no need for more complexity than that. On the other hand, kin and kinship became an important factor of one's personal identity. However, even that social trait had to evolve over time. With that in mind, we can delve into their process of transformation, which scholars have divided into three separate stages.

A size comparison of average humans with several extinct New Zealand bird species.
Source: Conty, CC BY 3.0 <https://creativecommons.org/licenses/by/3.0>, via Wikimedia
Commons https://commons.wikimedia.org/wiki/File:Dinornithidae_SIZE_01.png

The earliest of these stages is often referred to as the Archaic or Colonial. The less formal nickname was the Moa Hunter period, indicating one of the most important aspects of the early Māori culture. The moa is a family of flightless birds that lived in New Zealand; they were visually similar to ostriches. The largest of them grew up to 12 feet (3.6 meters) in height, and they weighed up to 510 pounds (230 kilograms). The smallest of the species were "only" as big as turkeys. As such, they were an ideal source of food, especially since prior to human arrival, they didn't have ground-based predators. Its only real threat was the Haast's eagle, whose wingspan reached up to three meters and weighed up to thirty-three pounds (fifteen kilograms). This made the moas easy prey for the early Māori hunters. Not only were these birds a superb source of food, but their large bones were also useful for fishhooks and harpoon heads, as well as various ornaments. Their large eggshells were useful for carrying water, while their feathers may have been used in clothing. Because of that, the early Māori hunted them in the tens of thousands over the years.

However, it would be wrong to assume that the Archaic period revolved solely around the moa. The Māori also hunted fur and elephant seals, sea lions, and dolphins, including the pilot whales, which are among the largest dolphin species in the world. They also fished and hunted smaller birds, like geese, rails, swans, and pelicans, which are all somewhat larger than most modern birds.

The Māori also never abandoned horticulture, which they brought from East Polynesia. They continuously cultivated paper mulberry, Pacific purple yam, taro, gourd, and, of course, *kumara*. It is worth pointing out that only the southernmost settlements were suitable for growing these crops. Apart from food, the Māori searched for available minerals for toolmaking. These varied in availability. Obsidian was found on Mayor Island, basalt came from Coromandel, and greywacke was found in the Hauraki Gulf. These places are all located on the North Island. The South Island provided chert and silcrete in the Otago region, while the Nelson area was the source of argillite and serpentine.

Because of the variability in locally available materials, prey, and other resources, the various Māori tribes traded with each other. The spread of various tools and materials across New Zealand is evident of this, leading to the conclusion that the Māori settlements were interconnected. Another important aspect of the Colonial period was a more mobile lifestyle. While the early Māori weren't fully nomadic, they were quite mobile. Their settlements usually consisted of a central base, one most likely linked with horticulture and toolmaking. Around that main site were a number of outposts and stations linked with other important activities, such as hunting, mineral gathering, fishing, or foraging. It seems that most if not all of the tribes migrated between these locations based on seasonal needs since whole communities partook in these activities. Individual specializations were not as pronounced at this time as in later periods. Understanding and utilizing various seasons for different tasks is also backed by archaeological findings of preserving foods for the winter period, like, for example, drying fish.

However, not every part of early Māori life revolved around work. There are signs of various social and communal activities, like tattooing or dart-throwing. It would be logical to assume that these leisure activities were more often practiced during the winter months when their workload would subside. In terms of material culture, tools and ornaments of the Colonial period retained their general Polynesian nature, meaning there were not many original Māori aspects integrated into them. Similarly, their homes most likely remained simple huts. They were built from locally available trees. Finally, the remains of the early Māori show they were quite healthy and well-fed. They ate, for the most part, a high-protein diet. This allowed them to have higher fertility rates than most other Polynesians, with an estimated four to five children per mother. This led to rapid population growth, despite the fact that their hardworking lifestyle meant that most Māori died by their late thirties. Unfortunately, other than these broad depictions based on archaeological findings, there aren't any other available sources. The Māori myths and genealogies (*whakapapa*) didn't delve into everyday life. They merely explained how they got to those lands and, in some cases, described discoveries and the names of places to justify tribal or personal authority over them.

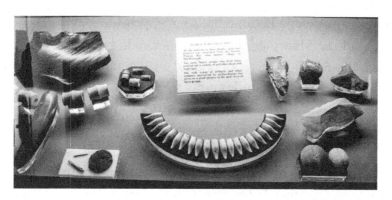

Some of the earliest and simplest Māori tools made from obsidian and bone dated to the Archaic period. Source: https://commons.wikimedia.org/wiki/File:Early_Maori_objects_from_Wairau_Bar,_Canterbury_Museum,_2016-01-27.jpg

Nevertheless, the Archaic or Moa Hunter period didn't last long. Most modern scholars estimate that within 100 or at most 150 years, the Māori managed to exhaust their large bird game. This was caused by reckless overhunting, which was additionally strained by the booming population. The demise of the moa and other large bird species was only hastened with the dogs and rats that came with the humans. If the grown specimens were too large for them, their defenseless eggs and younglings were fair game. Another contributing factor was habitat destruction. There are signs of great forest fires, which left many of the birds without shelter. It is unclear what caused these fires, but it seems they were most likely products of human activities. They may have been attempts to clear the land or to drive out prey from hiding places. They also might have been caused by nature, like, for example, by volcanic eruptions. It was most likely a combination of all these factors, though. In any case, most of these fires, natural or manmade, got out of control, sweeping large areas. By the mid- to late 14th century, the Colonial period came to an end, slowly evolving into the aptly named Transitional era.

The disappearance of their primary food sources forced the Māori to change their customs and way of life. Most notably, they had to refocus on their horticulture to survive. More land and time were used to grow crops, which slowly became their main source of nutrients.

Eventually, gardening became the source, providing up to 50 percent of the food the Māori ate. However, they didn't completely abandon hunting, though their targets became smaller birds, like kiwis, weka rails, pigeons, and other indigenous spices. Yet, since some of them were flighted birds, they were much harder to hunt, especially as the Māori lacked proper projectile weapons. Even when caught, these birds didn't provide as much food. Fishing and scavenging for shellfish also rose in importance, especially in regions where the climate wasn't as suitable for agriculture, as even the seal and sea lion populations were dropping due to extensive hunting. Foraging also became more important, and the Māori started utilizing more of the native plants, like nikau palms, various berries, and cabbage trees. Additionally, some scholars argue that during the Transitional period, the Māori started semi-cultivating some of the local vegetation, including cabbage trees, karakas or New Zealand laurels, and bracken ferns.

This prompted other major transformations, most notably a more sedentary lifestyle. Without big game, there was less incentive to roam between outposts. Additionally, larger gardens needed more care and discipline, so people had to stay in a single location. Coupled with that was the gradual advent of the Little Ice Age, prompting the Māori to stay more on the islands and worsening connections with the rest of the Polynesian world. Finally, they also devised a practice of preserving *kumara* in dugout storage pits. This meant the winter food supplies couldn't be moved, and if they were left alone, other tribes could easily raid them. Food scarcity and a larger population led to much fiercer competition for resources, making neighbors less friendly. To protect their own supplies, tribes began building small fortified hilltops known as *pā*, further making sedentary life an advantage. All of these aspects together forced the development of tribal social structures, with people gathering into one group with more distinctive divisions of labor. In turn, these larger organizations allowed the Māori to improve their activities, such as net fishing, gardening, and combat.

However, these changes didn't spread equally in the Māori world. Various groups adopted them at different times, with the southern tip of the South Island being among the last of them. The Māori of that region held on to the semi-nomadic lifestyle the longest since their climate wasn't as suitable for agriculture. Nevertheless, even on the North Island, different groups adopted this new lifestyle at different times. Yet, it was clear that those who were the first to adopt it benefited the most; in some cases, they even absorbed smaller and less developed tribes into their tribal organizations. With that, the Māori world slowly became less connected and friendly, with various tribes competing for resources and lands. The heightened rivalry of these groups may have caused some of the Māori groups to seek new homelands, spreading to other surrounding islands, like the Moriori of the previous chapter.

The Transitional period was also the time when the Māori culture began to noticeably differentiate from its East Polynesian roots. Their clothes were adapting to their new climate and the available materials on hand, like flax. Māori art began exhibiting new motifs and shapes, leading to unique art forms. Artisans started forming original Māori styles, most notably in the wood carvings and personal decorations, like, for example, *hei-tiki*, a pendant representing a human. During this period, these pendants started to appear in the form that is known today, with a tilted head and larger proportions in regards to its usually skinny body, as well as emphasized eyes. Additionally, the Māori began using greenstone or *pounamu*, most notably jade, serpentinite, or bowenite, for ornaments and jewelry. Another area where the Māori started to separate from their Polynesian roots is in their cultural memory. The Polynesians tended to pass on stories about their ancestors as a way to remember important deeds and moments of their shared past. As such, the stories of the first Māori settlers were distinctly tied with the people and events of the islands they came from. However, it was all preserved in oral tradition without a written language, making it rather susceptible to change.

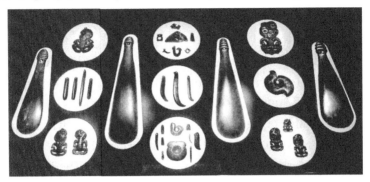

Collection of various pounamu objects, including several hei-tiki pendants.
Source: https://commons.wikimedia.org/wiki/File:Pounamu_objects,_Canterbury_Museum,_2016-01-27.jpg

The transformation of oral history, along with the Māori legends and mythology, began when the living Māori were several generations apart from their East Polynesian ancestors. By then, stories of their islands of origin and long separated kin became less important. These places and people weren't fully forgotten but instead became remembered as *Hawaiki*, which is "homeland" in Māori. It became a place of legends, linked with stories of their origin but without too many specific details. Their place was taken by more recent stories of migrations and explorations, which were more important for survival during the 14th and 15th centuries. Similarly, the general Polynesian mythology started to be adapted to local New Zealand needs and aspects. Folk tales, heroes, and places, which were brought from East Polynesia, were then linked and modified to represent the local lands of New Zealand, with stories that included native flora and fauna, events, and other features.

Overall, the Transitional period was when the indigenous Māori culture began to form, influence, and focus on their new homeland. This process was only helped by the growing isolation and separation from their Polynesian kin during the 15th century. With novel technologies and practices, different environments offering new food and materials, and spiritual and social divergence, the Māori shifted toward a unique and indigenous culture. By the early 16th century, the Māori society entered what scholars dubbed the Tribal period, finishing the formation of their distinctive civilization, sometimes called *Te Ao Māori* or the Māori worldview. Scholars also often refer to this era as the classical Māori age, as its hallmarks are mostly associated with the Māori civilization today.

Among these distinctive Māori characteristics, the tribal society was probably the most important. It was a culmination of the gradual transformation of the previous age, as the entire Māori population was divided into various tribes. Tribal membership was based on ancestry, and it was linked with either a founding forefather or even a foundational canoe. Thus, the highest and widest social group was called *waka*, which literally means canoe. However, by the 16th century, these familial ties were too distant to make *waka* a viable and coherent level of societal organization. Beneath it was *iwi*, which translates to bones or people, indicating a much closer connection among the members. In anthropological and Western terminology, *waka* could be identified as a phratry, while *iwi* would be a clan. In some cases, *iwi* could also be called *hapū*; however, in most cases, *hapū* was a subdivision of an *iwi*. It translates as pregnancy, indicating even closer blood relations. In a way, *hapū* was a sub-tribal division, sometimes even referred to as a tribal branch or a ramage. The lowest level of tribal division was the extended family or *whānau,* which literally means to give birth.

Of course, these divisions imply a theoretically tidy and organized society. Yet, life is rarely so simple. While *iwi* could bring several *hapū* together and work toward a common goal, every *hapū* had its own chief and operated separately on its own accord. Thus, *hapūs* of the same *iwi* could engage in internal conflicts. Similarly, not all *hapū* would join in an endeavor of their *iwi*. Another layer of complexity came from intertribal mixing. Despite the theoretical ancestral kinship as a prerequisite for membership, many individuals and families moved between *hapūs* and even *iwis*. These shifts could arise from various reasons, like marriages, adoptions, feuds, and even migrations. In some cases, a new *hapū* could be formed if the group grew too large for all families to continue living in a single area. In theory, this interchangeability between various clans and branches could be explained by shared ancestry through belonging to the same *waka*. Additionally, clan identity was also associated with *rohe pōtae* or tribal territory. Each *iwi* held dominion of certain lands, allowing people living within its boundaries to be acknowledged as its members.

Most of New Zealand was divided among the various *rohe*, whose borders were usually natural or geographical features. The most common markers were mountains, rivers, valleys, and forests. In some cases, a single identifiable tree or rock could be used as a dividing point. Authority over these lands was established and consolidated through the longevity of possession, the active utilization of its resources, or via conquest from its previous holders. Since dominion over the land was connected to spiritual beliefs, most notably mana or sacral authority, members of other tribes had to ask for permission to enter and use resources of lands that belonged to a different *iwi*. Failure to do so was a transgression significant enough to warrant an intertribal war. With tribal identity so closely linked with both ancestry and land, its expressions were commonly found in songs (*waiata*), chants (*patere*), and proverbs or mottos (*pepeha*). Additionally, the Māori *whakapapas* became even more important than before as records of familial ties and relations. All of these oral traditions were important for keeping track of tribal distinctions and changes, as well as for raising the sense of tribal unity and individuality.

The social stratification of the Māori didn't stop at the tribal level. A class hierarchy was established within each *hapū*. On a basic level, the Māori retained the basic divisions brought from their Polynesian ancestors. A minor group within a tribe was seen as *rangatira* or aristocrats, while most of its members were commoners or *tūtūā*. The basis of such divisions was based on personal mana, which was largely inherited from one's predecessors. However, personal deeds could further expand or diminish both individual and familial mana. In theory, there was a possibility that one could climb up the social hierarchy. Similarly, with enough offenses, a person could lose their rank.

The most distinguished member of a tribe could rise up to become *ariki* or chieftain. However, this position wasn't one of a singular ruler but more akin to a presiding member of the tribe. Nevertheless, due to their large mana, they were seen as people with the strongest connections to the gods, nature, and ancestors, making their thoughts and words the most notable and worthy. Thus, they carried a lot of influence. *Iwi* didn't have a united ruler, but individual *arikis* of each *hapū* were seen as equals, and they worked together when needed. However, in that context, there was an idea of a senior and junior *ariki*, which was based on their mana.

Besides the two main social groups, there were also recognized experts in various fields. These were the so-called *tohungas* or "chosen." Children that exhibited extraordinary talents were selected to be specially trained in some of the more notable skills by existing masters. These crafts could be more practical, like canoe builders or carvers, artful like tattooing, or spiritual like genealogy experts. *Tohunga* wasn't exactly a separate class, but even commoners that held this role were widely respected. Furthermore, mastery in such crafts was one of the ways an individual could gather more mana and rise up the social ladder.

Finally, there were the *taurekareka* or *mōkai*, a class of slaves beneath the *tūtūā*. These were most commonly captives from wars, but some were born into slavery. Of course, the *taurekareka* did most of the menial and hardworking jobs, but they weren't restrained too harshly. Loss of freedom was seen as a loss of mana, but regaining freedom through escape or honorable release restored their mana and former social standing. Similarly, children from marriages between slaves and free people would also be deemed free, as they would inherit mana from their free parent.

An 18ᵗʰ-century illustration of an unnamed Māori chief adorned by traditional tattoos. This drawing was made by a European visitor.
Source: https://commons.wikimedia.org/wiki/File:Maori_chief.jpg

It is worth noting that there were some divisions and differences between men and women. Some of the tasks and crafts were separated by gender. Tattoo artists and canoe builders were almost exclusively men. All spiritual crafts were also limited to men, as it was believed that women could contaminate the sacredness of such activities. However, some crafts, like weaving flax for clothes and floor mats, were exclusive to women. Female *tohungas* of high skill were seen as valuable members of society. In some tribes, women could play important roles in leadership and communal decision-making, but they could never become an *ariki*. Mana was inherited from and by both genders, yet in most cases, inheritance was based on the principle of male primogeniture.

Overall, there was a slight advantage in the social hierarchy for men, but women weren't as discriminated against in comparison to places like Europe. It should be mentioned that some European sources mention the mistreatment of wives by their husbands, but it doesn't seem to have been the norm. Additionally, in times of war, women weren't given any mercy by the enemy. They suffered torture and execution the same as men, even though they weren't active in the fighting. Similar treatment was seen with other "civilian" populations, like the elderly or children.

Because of the highly territorial nature of tribes and their unmerciful disposition toward their enemies, the classical Māori are often depicted today as violent and warlike. Supposedly, everything revolved around constant combat and revenge. However, that is an exaggeration made by later European writers. Most conflicts arose from individual or tribal transgressions, like, for example, encroaching or contesting a neighbor's land and resources or personal offenses that diminished someone's mana. Both of these offenses were seen as damaging to the concept of *utu*. Usually translated as revenge, its more accurate meaning is reciprocity or balance. This concept sat at the core of relations between both individuals and larger groups, such as families or tribes. It revolved around keeping the equilibrium of mana. Every favor had to be repaid with an equal favor, and every offense had to be rectified with a similar measure. Most writers tend to focus on the negative side of *utu*, in which the disbalance required martial compensation. However, that concept was also the basis for trade and cooperation between neighbors.

Yet, it is undeniable that *utu* led to various conflicts. Because mana was such an important idea among the Māori, leveling any debts or insults wasn't merely an option; it was seen as a necessity for the well-being of the entire tribe. This ensured there were plenty of reasons for war, especially because it could lead to a circle of perpetual violence. One tribe might see their attack as leveling the score, but the targeted *hapū* might interpret it as an insult to them because the record-keeping of *utu* wasn't universal but individual. In turn, this would lead to another retribution that could warrant even more reprisals. This is why some scholars tend to see *utu* as revenge. It is also important to note that these grievances were passed down by blood, like mana itself, leading to reprisals decades and generations after the initial offense. Sometimes the exact cause would be lost in time while the memory of it remained.

Even so, Māori warfare wasn't as endemic as it is portrayed. Fighting groups were often small, with primitive hand-to-hand weapons like clubs, staffs, or spears. The casualties were usually small. They also engaged in short campaigns that usually took place over the summer. The lack of portable preservable food made it difficult for these campaigns to last longer, and any long-term, substantial disruption of non-martial activities could jeopardize the survival of the tribe. Despite that, increased threats of conflict also meant that *pā* became more intricate than before, with ditches, palisades, and interior strongholds. A proper *pā* made any conquest and siege impossible. Yet, not every tribe had one. Ones that lived in more peaceful areas often didn't make or maintain their strongholds, while the tribes in more competitive regions had formidable forts. This unequal dissemination of *pās* is yet another indicator that war wasn't an omnipresent factor for all of the Māori. Especially since, in most cases, *pās* were a deterrent, a way to avoid more combat than necessary.

In times of peace, which were the most common when resources were abundant, Māori life was centered around gathering and growing food. Both tasks were done communally by both genders, with some separation of tasks. For example, men usually cleared the land and dug the soil, while women were often responsible for planting and weeding. Similarly, tasks of fishing, hunting, and cutting down trees were mostly done by men, while gathering berries and firewood as well as bringing fresh water were usually female tasks. Nevertheless, in most cases, tasks were done in groups and seasonally, depending on availability and the need for certain resources. A notable difference from the past eras was that by the Tribal period, the Māori had learned to preserve certain resources when they became scarce, preventing the extinction of more species.

Apart from food-related jobs, the Māori tribes spent ample time crafting tools and canoes and maintaining their forts and dwellings. These tasks were, in general, less communal, with some being carried out by *tohungas*.

Examples of Māori wood carvings from later periods.
Source: *https://commons.wikimedia.org/wiki/File:Tamatekapua.jpg*

Thanks to the distinctive separation of labor when it came to crafts, the classical Māori managed to achieve much higher sophistication in their arts than other Polynesians. Among the most notable crafts was carving (*toi whakairo*). Māori artisans most commonly carved wood, but they also worked with bones and stones. Jade and other types of greenstones were especially prized for jewelry, but they were also used to create carving tools. Common motifs were depictions of ancestors; some of these carvings were sacred and tied with tribal identity.

Tattoos (*tā moko*) played a similar role, with certain details representing personal achievements and milestones, while others were tied to one's lineage and status. Almost the entire body could be used for tattooing, but the most common places were the face, thighs, and buttocks for men and the chin, breasts, and neck for women. Backs were another common place for tattoos of both genders. The intricacy of tattoo patterns in the classical Māori period increased and surpassed most of the other Polynesians. To create these tattoos, they would use straight chisels instead of serrated ones, which had been used in previous periods. The punctures left small scars, creating a relief design on the skin. This scarred tissue added a new dimension to the basic two-dimensional paint patterns. Furthermore, Māori tattoos used both positive and negative pattern aspects, adding another layer of complexity.

In terms of quality of life, most Māori rarely lived beyond their thirties. Those who reached their forties became known as *kaumatua*, which literally translates as "no father," although it means an elder. It was an important status within a *whānau* or even wider. A person reaching their fifties was beyond exceptional, especially considering how tough Māori life was. A number of remains show signs of malnutrition at some point during their life, while from the late twenties onward, many would suffer from arthritis. Another common illness was gum infection and the loss of teeth, especially in their thirties, significantly shortening one's lifespan. This was caused by their diets, as they often ate fern roots and residual sand from shellfish. Another important notion is that functional Māori communities varied in size, from the smallest *whānau* to *hapū* with over five hundred people. They were usually settled near fresh water, food, and other resources. However, not all tribes were able to have all the things they needed in one location. Thus, the minority of them still moved and visited outposts, while others supplemented their deficiencies with trade.

Trade itself was based on the principle of *utu*, so the trade network was vast. There are signs of trade between the farthest points of the North and South Islands. The most commonly traded items were minerals since they were not found throughout all of the lands. Food was another important item, as tribes either tried to supplement their low reserves or sought items that weren't available in their region.

Local trade was done by foot, but for longer distances, the Māori used canoes. Though these were not ocean-worthy, they were suitable for sailing up the rivers or along the coast. These connections between tribes helped maintain peace, as it could alleviate shortages and unify the Māori world. Despite their tribal divisions and local differences, the Māori civilization remained homogenous. Disregarding separate tribal legends and genealogies, they continued to share common myths and belief systems. The Māori language also remained the same, though some local dialects appeared.

Thus, by the early 17th century, all of New Zealand was settled by Māori who shared common values. Their numbers may have been as high as 100,000 by the 18th century. They lived in a world of their own, as they were isolated from other people and influences. However, that would change.

Chapter 3 – Early Contact with the Europeans

For several hundred years, the Māori lived in isolation. They had even lost contact with their Polynesian kinfolk. Living separated for generations made their civilization unique, but it also made the Māori believe they were the only humans in the entire world, which for them consisted of the islands of New Zealand. However, that worldview would soon change.

Their first contact with the outside world came in late 1642 and early 1643, which are the first events in Māori history that we can precisely date. It was achieved by Dutch captain Abel Tasman, who sailed from Batavia (present-day Jakarta) under the flag of the Dutch East India Company. His employers sent him on an exploratory mission to find the supposed *Terra Australis Incognita* or Unknown Southern Continent, a theorized landmass that was thought to be in the center of the Pacific Ocean. More precisely, Tasman was sent to find valuable spices and metals. Tasman first sailed to Mauritius, then headed east across the Indian Ocean. Surprisingly, Tasman and his men managed to completely miss the southern shores of Australia, whose northern coast was already discovered. Instead, he reached an island that would become known as Tasmania, but he did not stop.

Instead, he proceeded farther east before reaching an island known to its inhabitants as *Te Waipounamu*.

Upon reaching the northwestern area of the South Island, the Dutch expedition sailed north before reaching the Golden Bay on the island's northern tip. There, the Europeans saw smoke from manmade fires. For them, it wasn't anything too strange, as various explorers and expeditions encountered local native tribes during their travels. Even the Dutch East India Company warned Tasman not to trust any indigenous people he may encounter. However, for the local Māori who saw two large masted ships enter their lands, it must have been an otherworldly sight. They saw technology beyond their imagination and people who looked different than them coming from what they thought was an infinite sea. It could be compared to what modern people might feel if we ever met extraterrestrials. Unfortunately, the precise emotions and details of these events cannot be recreated from Māori traditions. The *iwi* that lived in the region, Ngāti Tūmatakōkiri, was vanquished, and their tales were lost in struggles against other tribes.

Instead, we have to rely on stories left by Tasman, which seems reliable enough. According to these accounts, in the late hours of December 18th, the Māori sailed with two *wakas* to inspect the intruders. Upon reaching the European ships, the Māori began to yell and sound the trumpets. The Dutchmen responded with trumpets of their own, thinking it might be a way to establish friendly communication with the natives. It was impossible for them to know that the Māori were establishing mana and dominance; they were basically challenging the Europeans to a fight. After all, those strangers threatened to encroach on their claimed land, which was quite fertile. A similar exchange happened in the morning of the next day, which was interpreted by Tasman as friendly gestures. The European ships were then surrounded by seven Māori canoes. The Dutchmen used a small boat to communicate between their ships, but it was attacked by one Māori *waka*. They rammed the boat, killing four Europeans in their attack. The main ships fired their guns, trying to protect their crewmates, but their shots missed. This was enough for the Māori to retreat.

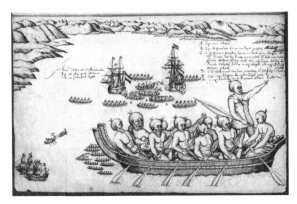

The earliest European depiction of the Māori made by Tasman's crewmember.
Source: https://commons.wikimedia.org/wiki/File:Gilsemans_1642.jpg

Upon realizing the hostility of the situation, Tasman decided to sail away in search of a suitable harbor and fresh water. However, as his ships prepared to set sail, twenty-two canoes began approaching them with great speed. It seems that the Ngāti Tūmatakōkiri felt they were winning, and they wanted to finish the altercation by gathering even more mana. As the leading *waka* came close enough, the Dutchmen opened fire once again, hitting a Māori warrior standing on the bow. He was supposedly holding a white flag. Another shot struck the side of a canoe, which persuaded the Māori to stop with their pursuit and return to land. It is possible that the Māori hit by the Europeans was a prominent member, if not the chief of the tribe, as its depiction by the expedition's artist shows him wearing a cape.

In any case, Tasman and his crew continued to sail northward along the western coast of the North Island. This shoreline presented no safe places to land, both because of its geography and because of poor weather. Upon reaching the northern tip of the island, they once again saw Māori on land, who reportedly stood on its ridges. They were shouting and throwing stones at them, but they did not try to reach the Europeans on their canoes.

This was enough for Tasman to abandon further inspection of the new lands, and he continued sailing north. On January 6th, 1643, the Dutch expedition left New Zealand. It later reached Fiji before sailing westward along the coast of New Guinea and then back to Indonesia. Both Tasman and his employers failed to see anything worthwhile in these obviously hostile new lands. Thus, they didn't follow up on these initial discoveries.

Nevertheless, the lands were entered into the Dutch East India maps. Originally, Tasman named it "Staten Landt" after the Dutch Parliament or the States General (*Staten-Generaal*). In fact, he believed it was the continuation of the land his countrymen had discovered in the early 17th century, one southwest of the South American coast. However, it was soon proved that the original South American Staten Landt was merely an island, prompting a name change. An unknown cartographer in the company renamed it Nieuw Zeeland or Nova Zeelandia in Latin. This was done to match the name of the western Australian coast, which was known as Nova Hollandia. (Zeeland and Hollandia were names of two neighboring provinces in the Netherlands.) Over time, Nova Zeelandia was eventually transcribed as New Zealand, the name that is associated with the islands today.

Tasman's discovery remained on record, but decades passed without further European expeditions to New Zealand. It was only 126 years later that another captain was ordered to explore the region. However, before we move from one European adventurer to another, it should be noted that the Māori continued to live as they had before Tasman's brief contact. His arrival was so unimportant that none of the other tribes mentioned it in their oral histories. More importantly, there were plenty of events among various *iwi* that were more important. Some tribal stories recall wars, conquests, migrations, and other notable events. Certainly, there were alliances, betrayals, and offenses of mana. Some Māori tribes built new forts, others cleared more lands, some new *iwi* and *hapū* formed, and others disappeared.

It would be unfair to the vibrant and changing Māori world to merely hop from one European contact to another without at least acknowledging this fact.

However, delving into more details about these events is beyond the scope of an introductory guide. There were dozens of tribes whose histories and memories vary in detail and quality. Piecing out proper intertribal relations would be a tedious process, filled with holes and guesses. Another issue is that the chronological details of Māori stories are passed down through the generations, so the stories change over time. Finally, even if there was a reliable way to compile all of the different stories into a coherent and understandable history, the end result would be too extensive, at least for this guide. With that in mind, the next major event in Māori history, one that truly changed their world for good, was the arrival of British explorer James Cook. He sailed on a single ship from England, heading first toward Tahiti to make some astronomical observations before going south in search of *Terra Australis Incognita* or until he reached the lands discovered by Tasman. Cook finally reached New Zealand (or New Zeland as it was called then) on October 6th, 1769.

His first encounter with the Māori went similar to Tasman's. On October 8th, Cook's vessel approached Poverty Bay (*Tūranganui-a-Kiwa*) on the eastern coast of *Te Ika-a-Māui*. It was greeted by a Māori war party performing one of their ceremonial challenges to the offenders who encroached on their mana. One of the sailors recognized the hostility of these actions and shot at them, killing one of the warriors. Another incident resulting in the death of a Māori man was recorded the very next day. In most cases, that would be enough for any European sailor to deem all locals a threat and deal with them aggressively. However, Cook was sent on explorations with an order to respect all indigenous people. Moreover, it seems that Cook himself shared the same belief. Even after these initial accidents, he still believed there was a way to create amicable relations with the Māori. His calmness, as well as his astute assessment that intimidation and bravado were an important part of this indigenous culture, helped to bridge the gap.

An important part of Cook's success in connecting with the Māori was the fact that on Tahiti, he took a Polynesian priest named Tupaia on as a crewmember. His services were quite useful for navigating the islands of Polynesia, but they were even more crucial for mutual understanding with the Māori. Though the dialects were different, as there had been several centuries of separate development, both East Polynesian and Māori languages were still similar enough for their speakers to understand each other. Thanks to that, most of the ensuing dealings between Cook and the Māori were cordial and respectful, allowing him and his crew to get familiar with indigenous customs over the next six months. During that time, Cook circumvented both major islands, even sailing up the Waihou River, which is located on the North Island. He and his men also explored some of New Zealand's interior, in some cases visiting Māori settlements. In other cases, they invited the Māori to board their ship.

Cook would return to New Zealand three more times, all during the 1770s, further expanding his knowledge and the reputation he had among the Māori. Like on his initial visit, he had Tahitian interpreters to help with communication, which didn't always prevent misunderstandings. On several occasions, there were altercations that led to the death of someone. However, Cook never jumped to the conclusion that the Māori were intrinsically to blame. For example, when ten of his crew members were killed in 1773, he personally investigated the reason, learning that one of his sailors had taken an adze from a Māori barterer but offered nothing in return. This violated *utu*, and it was enough reason for a deadly fight. Thus, Cook's disposition and behavior left him in fond memory of most Māori that met him. They recognized and often mentioned him as something similar to a *rangatira*, despite the fact that Cook was of lowly origins back in England. It is also worth noting that he wasn't merely learning about New Zealand and the Māori. He also taught his hosts that there was a much wider world around them. In fact, on one of his trips, he took two Māori with him back to the Society Islands. It was the first time the Māori reconnected with their long-forgotten ancestral lands.

A drawing made by Tupaia of a Māori man bartering crayfish with an English sailor for a piece of clothing.
Source:https://commons.wikimedia.org/wiki/File:A_Maori_man_and_Joseph_Banks_exchanging_a_crayfish_for_a_piece_of_cloth,_c._1769.jpg

Overall, Cook's voyages were instrumental for unlocking both New Zealand and the Māori to the rest of the world. By the end of the 18th century, there were a number of other explorers who visited the New Zealand archipelago. Most of them were either British or French, as both imperial powers had nearby colonies. Some were brief and unimpactful, while others existed for a longer period of time. However, Cook's expedition introduced the idea of an outside world and the idea of foreign visitors. The Māori were now more prepared to deal with the Europeans. Similarly, Cook's insight into Māori culture, especially their rituals and code of conduct, allowed those other interactions to be more amicable. At least some of the Europeans on those expeditions understood that despite their shouting and threatening dances, the Māori weren't necessarily hostile.

Nevertheless, this knowledge didn't stop misunderstandings and deadly altercations from happening. Probably the best example is the visit of the French privateer Marc-Joseph Marion du Fresne in 1772. He and his crew anchored in the Bay of Islands on the northern tip of the North Island. Initially, the Māori of the Ngāpuhi *iwi* were friendly with the visitors. The French sailors learned about the Māori life, exchanged visits, and bartered. However, after several weeks of amicable relations, several hundred Māori warriors attacked the French camp on the shore. Marion and twenty-six of his sailors were killed in an attack, which provoked a retaliation that leveled an entire Māori village. Up to three hundred Māori were killed, with more wounded on both sides. From the French perspective, it was an unprovoked attack. However, from the Māori perspective, the visitors infringed on the *tapu* (sacredness or holiness) of the bay. It was a concept that was as important as *utu* or mana, and it revolved around the prohibition of profane involvement in some action or place. Thus, when the European visitors went against *tapu*, the Māori were obliged to punish them to appease the gods.

This and other similar clashes proved to be vital for the Māori in the long term. Despite Cook's depiction of them as noble, brave, and open, as well as often benevolent, deaths of European sailors brandished them as inconsistent, unreliable, and even treacherous. More importantly, the Māori were seen as vigorous, organized, and martially capable. Subduing and controlling them in a colonial enterprise in what was still quite extensive geographical isolation was not going to be easy. Thus, the Europeans, most notably the British, decided to forego any colonial plans in the region. Instead, they focused on Australia, whose Aboriginal population was seen as less troublesome. For several decades, until the early 19th century, the Māori world was merely a place for exploration and trade. This allowed the Māori to learn and adapt to new technologies and knowledge brought by the Westerners, at least to some degree.

Initially, the most notable imports from the Māori perspective were metal tools and new foods. They were more than eager to trade for nails, which they could use as chisels or fishhooks. Other metal objects were also praised. However, over time, they also began showing an increased interest in muskets and other weapons, as they could shift favor and the power balance in their intertribal conflicts. Another important import was potatoes, as well as other root vegetables like turnips. These quickly spread across the Māori world as an important food source. With them came new agricultural tools as well as some new fruits, creating a more balanced diet. Along with these, they showed interest in European clothes as well as the concept of literacy. In general, the Māori were willing to learn and experiment with almost anything the Europeans had to offer. They would test and experiment on new materials and tools, trying to find a way to utilize them for their own need. Sometimes, these uses would be surprising to the Westerners. The useless items were discarded, while the useful ones were adopted in manners coherent with Māori values and ideas.

Despite that influence, for a long period, the European presence didn't change much in terms of Māori life and traditions. They merely brought new materials, food, and items that the tribes fitted in their existing worldviews. However, the Māori civilization wasn't impregnable to change and foreign influence. At the close of the 18th and start of the 19th century, New Zealand's remoteness decreased due to new sailing technologies. The nearby lands were also colonized by Western powers. Furthermore, New Zealand had resources coveted by those nations, mainly timber and flax, which were needed to sustain the growing imperial navies. Along with that were sea mammal oils and fats, as well their skins.

However, the European influence on the Māori didn't initially come from planned colonization but rather from individual sailors who escaped their service and ships for various reasons. These Europeans sought shelter with the Māori and were accepted with great hospitality. Their hosts cloistered these escapees from their troubles.

In return, the foreigners passed on their knowledge and expertise in trades and crafts. Most notable were their contributions to horticulture and animal husbandry. The sailors also acted as mediators and interpreters when other Europeans came to trade with the Māori. However, instead of trying to "civilize" their Māori hosts, they accepted all of their traditions. They accepted the ideas of kinship ties and mutual balance, and they partook in combat and ceremonies. They even took wives and interconnected with the Māori society to the fullest. On rare occasions, they even marked themselves with Māori tattoos. Some of them even produced offspring that continued to live among the Māori. Because of their integration, they became known as Pākehā Māori, which would be translated as "foreign Māori."

It is important to note that the term "Pākehā" is today translated as foreigner or alien, and it usually has a connotation of either all non-Māori or, more commonly, New Zealanders of European or non-indigenous descent. However, the etymology of the word is lost. Some scholars link it with the mythical *pakepakehā*, supernatural beings with pale skin and blond or red hair. However, the problem is that the name of these creatures is more commonly *patupaiarehe*, making it questionable to link the term to foreigners. Others have linked it with various forms of words, such as pig, producing a more derogatory meaning of "white pig" or "pig flea." However, this theory is filled with conjectures and is widely regarded as incorrect.

Furthermore, most Māori speakers claim the term isn't derogatory or malicious and that it doesn't usually have negative connotations. In any case, the etymology behind the term *Pākehā* isn't as important and may have been lost to history. Yet it is important to note that even today, the Māori use it for foreigners and non-indigenous New Zealanders. Even some of the non-Māori New Zealanders use the term *Pākehā* when referring to themselves.

In any case, there weren't that many Pākehā Māori. By the 1830s, there were an estimated seventy of them in total. Thus, their influence was limited but valuable for the Māori. More important and influential were the actual colonists. English seal hunters could be marked as the forebearers of colonialization in New Zealand. They would exchange seal skins for tea with Chinese traders. As early as 1792, a group of them was dropped off in the Dusky Sound (*Tamatea*), a fiord in the southwestern corner of the South Island. However, seal hunter colonies weren't permanent; they were usually abandoned within a year. Furthermore, they were usually built in more remote regions, making their interaction with the Māori rather limited. The peak of seal hunting came in the first decade of the 19th century, by which time even the Māori became crewmembers on seal hunting expeditions. They traveled with the Europeans as well as Tahitians and Aboriginal Australians. These men brought back secondhand knowledge about the world and European technologies to their tribes. At the same time, some of the seal traders ran off to the surrounding Māori tribes to grow pigs and vegetables to trade with other Pākehā that visited the southern tip of *Te Waipounamu*. They, too, usually became integrated into the Māori society, becoming Pākehā Māori.

Kororareka Beach, Bay of Islands, 1844.

An illustration of Kororāreka, the first European colony in New Zealand, which was established in the 1840s.
Source: Archives New Zealand from New Zealand, CC BY-SA 2.0
<https://creativecommons.org/licenses/by-sa/2.0>, via Wikimedia Commons
https://commons.wikimedia.org/wiki/File:Koror%C4%81reka_(Russell),_1844_(173865103.9 1).jpg

However, like the early Māori, the sealers were too efficient in hunting their prey. By the 1810s, they had basically overexploited the seals, making seal hunting mostly unprofitable, with the exception of a brief resurrection in the mid-1820s. Despite that, thanks to whaling, the Pākehā remained a constant presence in the Māori world. They first developed ocean whaling, which started simultaneously as sealing. However, it did not reach its peak until the 1830s. As the number of whaling ships rose, they began using the Bay of Islands as a natural harbor. The local Māori saw value in bartering with them, leading to the creation of Kororāreka (modern-day Russell). It was a mixed settlement of both Pākehā and Māori. It became an early melting pot of the Māori and European worlds. However, since the Western sailors were usually lowlifes, the result of this mixing earned Kororāreka as the name of "Hellhole of the Pacific." Besides providing the Pākehā with food and timber, Kororāreka Māori also offered them alcohol and prostitutes. Due to the lack of laws or policing, the atmosphere in the town became increasingly disorderly.

Despite that, ocean whaling had a more limited effect on the Māori since it was mostly localized to Kororāreka.

More widespread interaction came with shore whaling in the 1820s. This type of whaling meant that the Pākehā built a number of hunting stations along the eastern coast of both major islands, as well as on the Cook and Foveaux Straits. More importantly, these settlements were usually established near Māori villages. In some cases, the Māori moved their homes closer to the Pākehā. In these small mixed communities, the Pākehā and the Māori worked together, prompting much closer interactions. The Māori were introduced to more of the European technologies, as well as tools, animals, plants, and Western-styled clothing and housing. Of course, there was a significant number of intermarriages, and the Māori became increasingly exposed to the English language. Nonetheless, these communities retained their Māori traditions, values, and culture. Even the children of mixed marriages identified as Māori, despite having Pākehā surnames. These whaling societies were examples of Māori-Pākehā symbiotic relations. The Europeans gained access to much-needed raw materials and help to achieve greater profits. In return, the Māori gained access to additional labor during the off-season, as well as Western technologies and knowledge without compromising their Māori cultural identity. It is also worth noting that these hunting stations were able to form only because the Māori permitted their existence, as it benefited them.

Another important area was the timber industry. Despite New Zealand's vast forests, the Europeans initially saw little value in most local trees. However, by the 1820s, they discovered the kauri, a tall tree that was flexible and strong and did not have too many branches on its trunk. It was perfect for masts and beams. Once again, the Pākehā were more than glad to employ Māori workers to help them with labor, adding yet another influx of foreign influence on their societies. Coupled with that was the harvesting and weaving of flax, which turned out to be one of the most sought-after products of the

Māori. It was used for ropes, sails, nets, and sacks, which are all essential for maritime industries.

To a lesser extent, the Māori also produced pigs and various fruits that were exported by some of the European traders to Australia and other nearby English colonies. Besides that, the Westerners recognized that the Māori came from a maritime culture; thus, they recruited them for their ships. Some of them sailed all around the globe, reaching both the United States and England by 1810. The Māori also became regular visitors of Australian harbors. They were slowly being introduced to the world, as the world was with them.

However, this mixing with the Pākehā didn't mean that the Māori were losing their own identity. While they were more than glad to trade their resources and labor for liquor or tools, their main goal was getting their hands on muskets. Beneath all of their interactions with the Europeans lay their traditional intertribal competition. If one tribe received new weapons, the other needed to procure them as well. Similarly, the Māori never abandoned their basic ideals of mana or *utu*. They only accepted foreign ideas, knowledge, and technologies as long as they could be placed within the concept of their world. In fact, in these early decades, it seems that the Māori were able to entice more Europeans to "convert" than the other way around. The English authorities in Australia even tried to further the supposed "civilization" of the Māori by hosting various chiefs for a prolonged time. Besides hoping to receive similar invitations based on the principle of reciprocity, they hoped that their "civilized qualities" would trickle down from the chiefs to their subordinates. However, the Māori civilization proved largely immune to such colonizing attempts.

In the end, despite their large civilizational differences, the Māori and the Pākehā managed to live in relative harmony and peace. There were no major clashes, merely some localized incidents and misunderstandings. Most surprising was the fact that the Māori proved to be more than capable of competing in almost any field with the supposedly superior Europeans. However, their resilience and abilities were soon to be tested by the much more organized English invaders.

Chapter 4 – Turbulences, Wars, and Colonization

The arrival of the Pākehā changed many aspects of Māori life, bringing new materials, technologies, and knowledge. However, in the early period of interaction with the foreigners, some core aspects of *Te Ao Māori* remained the same. One of them was intertribal conflicts.

Despite retaining relative peace with the Europeans, the Māori never stopped warring with each other. Tribal competition for resources and mana was always an important part of their life. While the Pākehā didn't directly change that, they did alter the way these conflicts were fought. They brought muskets to the Māori, which rose in abundance. By the early 19th century, they were mass-produced, making them cheaper. The Māori initially used them for hunting, as new ranged firearms made it significantly easier to kill smaller birds. However, it wasn't long before they realized the enormous potential of that weapon for warfare. Surprisingly, the inaugural use of muskets was a failure. In 1807 or 1808, the Ngāpuhi and Ngāti Whātua tribes clashed in the Battle of Moremonui, north of modern-day Dargaville. The former had some guns, but the Ngāti Whātua warriors ambushed them, giving them little time to reload. Despite the

Ngāpuhi loss, the Māori saw how much potential lay in the new weapon, especially if it was employed in larger numbers. From then on, the use of firearms began to spread among the various tribes, starting what the modern historians have dubbed the Musket War, a period lasting for about thirty years.

A mid-19th century illustration depicting Māori warriors with muskets and their traditional weapons. Source: https://commons.wikimedia.org/wiki/File:Thomas_John_Grant_-_War_dance_-_Google_Art_Project.jpg

The spread of firearms was slow and uneven. Some *iwis* had more foresight and opportunities to acquire them, while other tribes were less fortunate. Thanks to that disbalance of power, the ensuing conflicts became increasingly ferocious and deadly. The first tribe to dedicate its resources to trade for guns was the Ngāpuhi *iwi*, located in what is today the Northland Region of New Zealand and centered in the Hokianga and the Bay of Islands. Despite the loss near Moremonui, their new chief Hongi Hika, who gradually rose to power after the battle, understood the advantage muskets could bring on the battlefield. He encouraged all who recognized his mana to grow crops that were used to barter for firearms, slowly building up the Ngāpuhi arsenal. In 1815, he became the leader of the entire *iwi*. By 1817, he began his first campaign, raiding surrounding tribes who stood no chance against his better-armed and trained Ngāpuhi musketeers. Over the next couple of years, his raids brought about a considerable number of slaves, which allowed him to increase his production and capability to procure more firearms. Victories, trade, and friendly relations with the Pākehā missionaries skyrocketed Hongi's reputation enough for him to visit both Australia and England as a guest of the British Crown.

While on his journey, Hongi met with British King George IV and learned about the Pākehā culture, but he also taught the British about the Māori civilization. Hongi even helped with creating the first Māori-English dictionary. Along the way, he received many gifts, including a suit of armor given to him by the king. However, on his way home, he exchanged most of these gifts for more muskets, bringing some five hundred guns back to his tribe. In late 1821, Hongi and the Ngāpuhi continued their campaign with even greater force, as by then, they had at least one thousand muskets. Over the next several years, the Ngāpuhi took revenge on all the surrounding tribes, even for slight grievances from the past. In most cases, their enemies either had no or very few guns of their own, making them an easy target. By that time, some other southern tribes acquired enough firepower for themselves, and they began similar raids. By 1822/23, the Māori Musket Wars had swept all of New Zealand, with small exceptions of the distant mountainous interior and the southernmost fiord region.

These clashes intensified, rising in brutality and cruelty, as balancing *utu* became bloodier than before. Hongi himself lived into his fifties, dying in 1828. His longevity was in part due to the armor he received from the British king, as it saved his life on at least one occasion. Nevertheless, his death didn't bring any respite in the wars, and they continued to rise in intensity, reaching a peak in 1832/33.

It should be pointed out that the muskets were only part of the equation needed for such widespread fighting. The other mastering the cultivation of the potato. It gave more nutrition to the Māori, and it also lasted longer than other foodstuffs. In turn, this allowed larger, longer, and more distant campaigns to take place, including sieges of previously impregnable *pās*. Over time, the Musket Wars caused great turbulence, with some smaller tribes perishing or nearing extinction. Many others migrated, escaping from their more powerful enemies and in turn spreading the seeds of war by attacking other *iwis* they encountered. Some of the tribes even sailed to the Chatham Islands, killing some 10 percent of the Moriori population and enslaving the rest.

However, by 1836, the fighting began to die down. This was due to several reasons. First and foremost, all the surviving tribes acquired enough muskets to make further raids less worthwhile to the attackers. A new balance of power among the tribes was achieved. Furthermore, by then, the European presence and the buying of lands began to stabilize the extent of tribal *rohes* while also blocking further migrations and conquests. Nevertheless, some clashes did occur in the following years, with the last probably being the fight between the Ngāti Mutunga and Ngāti Tama on the Chatham Islands in 1840.

Even after that, there was a constant threat of musket-armed war parties, but the all-out warfare died down. By then, some twenty thousand Māori had lost their lives, with many more enslaved or displaced. This makes the Musket Wars one of the deadliest events in Māori history. Nevertheless, despite the scope of destruction being directly caused by European technology, these wars were, in fact, the continuation of previous Māori traditions of intertribal warfare. They were, in essence, part of the Māori legacy, and it was only fueled by more advanced weaponry.

Another important factor in ending the prolonged intertribal violence was the spread of Christianity, which brought its theoretical messages of peace and love. Regardless, the process of adopting this foreign faith wasn't quick or straightforward. Any early attempts to convert the Māori were impossible, as the Westerners needed to learn their language and create much-needed dictionaries. Thus, the first mission was set up only in 1814 by the Church of England in the Bay of Islands. Members of this mission were instructed to first "spread civilization," which meant teaching the Māori about agriculture, technology, and trade, as well as European morals and manners. However, the missionaries were far from the saints they tried to teach the Māori. They indulged in drunkenness and adultery, and they even propagated the musket trade. In fact, since they lived in the Ngāpuhi *rohe*, Chief Hongi became quite friendly with them for that reason. He protected them without ever converting himself. With that in mind, it seems that the early missionaries actually helped to fuel the Musket Wars and gave the Ngāpuhi these much-coveted weapons.

Nevertheless, by the early 1820s, the interaction between the missionaries and the Māori changed. Firstly, the Church of England expanded the missions and altered its policies. Its members were banned from trading in weapons, and preaching became the priority over "civilizing." All of the missionaries had to learn the Māori language and start explaining the core tenets of Christianity. As the language barrier was becoming less of an issue, the dialogue between the Māori and the Pākehā missionaries began. As quite spiritual and religious people, the Māori proved to be unexpectedly open to discussions about faith. They already believed there were *atua*, supernatural forces or beings in nature. Some were more akin to deities and ancestors, while others were like demons or spirits. They also believed in the existence of a soul (*wairua*) that was separate from the body, as well as the already mentioned *tapu* and the general belief that everything in nature and life was in some way connected. Furthermore, the Māori followed their own set of rules, codes, and customs known as *tikanga*, which was largely based on their religious beliefs.

Māori chiefs (the middle is Hongi Hika) with a Christian missionary. Source: https://commons.wikimedia.org/wiki/File:The_Rev_Thomas_Kendall_and_the_Maori_chiefs_Hongi_and_Waikato,_oil_on_canvas_by_James_Barry,.jpg

Thus, in general terms, their spiritual principles weren't too far away from some ideas of Christianity. Soul, sacredness, set of religious laws—they held all of that in common. There are some indications that a few of the tribes already believed that there was some supreme being above all humans and *atua* called Io. This means that accepting the singular Christian God was possible due to their preexisting beliefs.

Nevertheless, there were some large contrasts as well. For example, the Māori had a hard time accepting the idea that humans were fallen creatures in need of salvation and redemption. Even more troublesome was the concept that in the eyes of God and his followers, all human life was equal, be it a commoner, an aristocrat, or even a slave. That went against the core mana principles, where one's worth was acquired and accumulated over time. Despite that, it seems that this Christian rejection of the institution of slavery proved to be a much-needed step in expansion. Many of the early Māori evangelists were, in fact former, Ngāpuhi slaves who spread the word of Christ when allowed to return to their own *iwis*.

Coupled with that was the fact that by the 1820s, other Christian denominations sent their own missionaries to New Zealand. Their success varied, but they spread the ideas and tenets of Christianity. Another important factor was the spread of literacy and the increased production of scriptures, once again spreading the reach of the Pākehā faith. Yet, all that would have had less of an impact if the Māori world hadn't been as shaken. By the 1830s, many of the Māori felt less secure in their own beliefs, as they had been confronted with large-scale death and destruction from the Musket Wars. The spread of European diseases brought by the whalers also caused great losses. Some saw a possible solution in the new religion, and the number of Māori Christians rose to several thousand by the early 1840s.

However, many of the converted Māori never fully accepted Christianity. Instead, they accepted the part of it that they felt close to and which they "needed." The Māori were essentially converting Christianity to fit their own purposes than actually converting. This gave birth to a number of syncretic religions and movements that combined Māori and Christian beliefs to form a unique, more Māori path to salvation and God.

However, their defensive and resistant nature was possible as long as the Europeans remained only sporadically interested in New Zealand. Indeed, since the late 1780s, the only European authorities that took a constant interest in the ongoings of the Māori world were governors of the New South Wales colony centered in Sydney. This meant that the Māori had some fifty years of gradual engagement with the Pākehā on their own terms. They weren't overwhelmed by European imperialism and colonialism like many other indigenous peoples around the world. However, by the 1830s, thanks to their closeness and existing economic ties, the British Crown became interested in expanding its control over New Zealand. The heightened interest came from the British government's worries that the Musket Wars and turbulence caused by it might threaten the lucrative trade between Australia and New Zealand. Furthermore, by then, there was a growing number of British subjects living among the Māori who lacked any protection or laws. On top of that, some of the Māori tribes even asked the British king for protection, both from their British subjects and the visiting French military.

That was enough enticement for the British government, which always sought new avenues and places to expand its empire and revenue. The Musket Wars provided fertile soil for Britain's gradual push into the Māori world. After more than two decades of large-scale conflicts, accompanied by illnesses brought by sporadic and localized contact with the Europeans, the Māori population dropped to an estimated seventy thousand. The wars also displaced many tribes, creating additional confusion and feelings of anxiety. However, the British approached their goal in New Zealand with tact and diplomacy instead of with blazing guns. They sent James Busby as a representative of the Crown in 1833. Upon his arrival, he brought gifts to a number of chiefs, starting his mission of safeguarding both the British and the Māori. Busby tried to defuse the relations on the islands, but he lacked any authority to back his actions, making them rather fruitless.

The more important part of his mission was to persuade the Māori to accept an idea of a more structured and European-styled government that would represent all the tribes. Busby first gathered a number of northern chiefs to create a flag design for New Zealand's ships, which they did after some misunderstandings. The entire ordeal was outside of Māori cultural understandings or necessity. It represented the unity of the tribes as a single entity, which was still a foreign concept in Māori society. With that in mind, it became known as the Flag of the Independent Tribes of New Zealand. The following year, this concept was further expanded when Busby and his associates drew up the Declaration of Independence of New Zealand. It proclaimed the independence of the so-called United Tribes of New Zealand, with sovereignty and authority residing with the hereditary tribal chiefs and their assembly. Along the way, the document asked King William IV to act as the protector or *matua* (parent) of the supposed Māori state.

Just over fifty chiefs signed the declaration, but like the flag, it was largely a foreign concept. The minority may have seen it as a way to gain the upper hand in their intertribal conflicts, while some possibly had some economic and trade interests. However, the idea of a federal Māori state was beyond their political concepts. Similarly, the rest of the British government saw Busby's declaration as insignificant nonsense that ran against their plans in the region. As such, for the most part, the declaration remained a dead letter. Yet, it represents the first step toward constitutionalized relations between the Māori and the British Crown, as well as the basis of indigenous rights. London's dissatisfaction with Busby's work finally prompted the British government to send a new representative, William Hobson, to New Zealand. He had only one task: secure the legal transfer of sovereignty from the Māori to the British Empire.

Hobson arrived in the Bay of Islands on January 29th, 1840. He immediately began work on drawing up a legal document to fulfill his urgent mission. It was done by February 4th, but the end result was of dubious quality. Neither Hobson nor his assistants were lawyers, and the British Colonial Office didn't provide them with a draft of the document. If the quality of the document was questionable in its original tongue, additional problems arose when Hobson gave it to the missionaries to translate. He knew that if the Māori chiefs were to understand it, debate it, and accept it, the treaty had to be in their native language. The translation was done within a day, and on February 5th, Hobson gathered the Māori leaders in front of Busby's house and presented them with the so-called Treaty of Waitangi (*Te Tiriti o Waitangi*), named after the estuary river that ran near the gathering.

The text represented a shift in the imperial policy toward New Zealand. It was no longer acceptable to create a Māori land with accommodations and places for European settlers. Instead, they wanted to form a settler New Zealand while keeping some space for the Māori. Nevertheless, the wording of the treaty echoed Busby's earlier agreements. Thus, the preamble states that Queen Victoria is "anxious" and willing to protect "the Native Chiefs and Tribes of New Zealand" as a favor to secure their peace and order as a consequence of the rapid emigration of her subjects from Europe and Australia. According to the text, the queen wanted to create a settled form of civil government and to "avert evil" that comes from the lack of laws and institutions. It also states that the queen authorized Hobson to negotiate with the chiefs "for the recognition of Her Majesty's Sovereign authority over the whole or any part of those islands." The preamble concludes with an invitation to the "confederated and independent" chiefs to concur with the articles of the treaty.

A later painting depicting the signing of the Treaty of Waitangi.
Archives New Zealand from New Zealand, CC BY 2.0
<https://creativecommons.org/licenses/by/2.0>, via Wikimedia
Common*https://commons.wikimedia.org/wiki/File:%E2%80%9CThe_Signing_of_the_Treaty_of_Waitangi%E2%80%9D,_%C5%8Criwa_Haddon_-_Flickr_-_Archives_New_Zealand.jpg*

The first article was the most important for the British, as it called for the Māori chiefs, both of the United Tribes and the independent ones, to cede "absolutely and without reservation all the rights and powers of Sovereignty" over their territories to the queen of England. The second article proceeded to guarantee "the full exclusive and undisturbed possession of their Lands and Estates Forests Fisheries and other properties" to the chiefs and tribes of New Zealand. Yet, at the same time, that article affirms that the Crown and its representatives had exclusive rights to buy Māori lands if the owners decided to "alienate" their possession. Finally, the last article concisely states that the queen "extends to the Natives of New Zealand Her royal protection and imparts to them all the Rights and Privileges of British Subjects." The treaty closes with a clause that the Māori chiefs "made fully to understand the Provisions of the foregoing Treaty, accept and enter into the same in the full spirit and meaning thereof."

The English version on its own is somewhat vague and convoluted, but the Māori rendition suffers even more. The translation was rushed, and the document needed to convey ideas and concepts that the Māori language and civilization lacked. Most notable was the divergence in the notion of sovereignty. Both of these facts led to the Māori versions of the treaty differentiating from its original English form. Thus, in the Māori Treaty of Waitangi, the chiefs gave away their *kāwanatanga*, a loan translation from "governorship." In Busby's previous documents, the translation of sovereignty was mana, as in authority over something. Yet, even that wasn't an appropriate translation since the concept behind the two words was different, and mana isn't something that can be given up. Furthermore, in the translation of the second article, the chiefs retained "unqualified exercise of their chieftainship [*rangatiratanga*] over their lands, villages and all their treasures." Such wording gave the chiefs much broader powers. In fact, according to some modern scholars, the closest translation of sovereignty was *rangatiratanga*.

With that in mind, the literal understanding of the Māori translation would amount to the chiefs agreeing to hand over their rights of the governorship of New Zealand to the queen while retaining their sovereignty and authority over their own affairs and territories. Additional confusion is brought by the use of the word *taonga*, which means "treasures" or "precious things" in place of "other properties" in the wording of the second article. The Māori used *taonga* in a much broader term than the legal concept of property in English, encompassing the less tangible things such as culture, material or not, and language. Finally, the ending clause stipulates a full understanding of the treaty's spirit, which very few Māori could even try to do. The basic European notion of sovereignty was foreign to them, and very few Pākehā understood concepts of mana or other ideas of the Māori civilization.

Regardless of that, on February 5th, Hobson gathered several hundred Māori, including a few dozen chiefs, various Christian missionaries, and a number of local Pākehā. The latter were there merely as witnesses of the whole ordeal. When the Māori version was read to the chiefs and their followers, the missionaries who presented it tried to explain some of the concepts and terms of the treaty but not in precise terms. They intentionally emphasized the benevolence and protection offered to the tribes. One of them even told the Māori the treaty was an expression of love from Queen Victoria. It is clear that most missionaries, including the French Catholics, believed the treaty would work in their favor, while some might have even truly felt that it was in the best interests of the Māori to sign it. Thus, pretty much all of the Europeans present hoped for a quick and easy resolution.

Despite what the Pākehā wanted, the Māori chiefs weren't going to approach the matter lightly. They began a lengthy discussion among themselves. Initially, most of them were negative. For example, Chief Rewa of the Ngāpuhi *iwi* reminded his fellow chiefs that they were not foreigners and that they, the chiefs, were the governors of their ancestral lands. Similarly, Te Ruki Kawiti of the Ngāti Hine *hapū* argued the Māori were free and wanted to remain such, pressuring the Europeans to go back home. Moka Te Kainga-mataa, Rawa's brother, argued that the governor wouldn't actually have enough authority to fulfill the promise and asked Hobson for the land that had been unlawfully taken from him. At that point, it seemed the treaty was doomed to fail. However, the nature of a Māori tribal discussion was that both the positive and negative sides had to be heard.

Picture of Tāmati Wāka Nene taken in the 1870s
Source: https://commons.wikimedia.org/wiki/File:TamatiWakaNene1870s.jpg

Illustration of Te Ruki Kawiti from the 1940s.
Source: Archives New Zealand from New Zealand, CC BY-SA 2.0
<https://creativecommons.org/licenses/by-sa/2.0>, via Wikimedia Commons
https://commons.wikimedia.org/wiki/File:Te_Ruki_Kawiti_of_Ng%C4%81puhi_(160886628 23).jpg

Among the loudest was Hōri Kīngi Te Wharerahi, Moka's and Rawa's third brother, who proclaimed that the governor would bring peace to the Māori. His speech marked the turning of the tides, and he was helped by another Ngāpuhi chief named Tāmati Wāka Nene, a relative of Hongi Hika. Nene told his fellow chiefs that they had to have sent the Pākehā away when they first arrived. He argued that it was too late now. In fact, they needed a governor to act as a father, peacemaker, and judge among the tribes. However, Nene also declared that the governor had to preserve Māori land and customs. Both Nene and Wharerahi had considerable mana, and their words carried a lot of weight, allowing the positive stance to slowly take over. Nevertheless, an agreement wasn't reached during the day, and the Māori discussion continued throughout the night. It was only on the morning of February 6th that the majority of the chiefs accepted the treaty. At that moment, forty-five Māori chiefs signed their names or, in the case of the illiterate majority, drew their facial *moko* patterns.

However, before the signing ceremony was carried out, a French Catholic missionary prompted Hobson to tell the Māori that they wouldn't be persecuted based on their religion. He did this to protect his Catholic followers from the British Protestant government. Hobson agreed, as he just wanted to get the signing over with. Yet, this point was conveyed only vocally. Another missionary spoke to the Māori in their language, stating that the governor said the "several faiths," including various Christian denominations and "also Māori custom," would be protected by the government. This late verbal addition prompted later scholars to argue that this statement should be considered as the fourth article, one that allowed the freedom of religion. This adds another layer of confusion, leading to much debate among academics. According to some, from the perspective of European legality, the statement only carried moral obligation and weight but was legally unbinding. Others claim that in an oral society such as the Māori, an unwritten promise had the same weight as the written text.

Yet, in reality, this debate only became important in later periods, when the Māori struggled against New Zealand's government for their rights. During the Treaty of Waitangi, it was largely irrelevant to the Māori chiefs, who once again didn't really understand what the idea behind the freedom of religion was, nor how important it could be. Similarly, other discrepancies between ideas of sovereignty and mana or *rangatiratanga*, the questions of cultural preservation, and the differences between the English and Māori versions weren't important at that time. The chiefs only debated about accepting foreign domination, and they based their argument solely on the text presented to them in the Māori language. All of the debates behind the "true meaning" and issues of legality came later when bilingual scholars educated in the law began inspecting the treaty in its entirety. Even the New Zealand government in the late 20th century admitted that the document was plagued with many holes, saying that its weight was actually in its proclaimed spirit, not the actual text.

Despite that, the Treaty of Waitangi served Hobson's purposes. To further strengthen the agreement with the Māori, he also circulated several written copies, which were subsequently signed by other chiefs who weren't present. Interestingly, among the signers of the original were also the chiefs who opposed the treaty. Some simply accepted the wishes of the majority, while others were pressed by their tribe. Nevertheless, within several months, over five hundred signatures had been gathered. Even before this final number was reached, Hobson felt enough had been gathered for him to finally proclaim British sovereignty of New Zealand on May 21st, 1840. Officially, in the eyes of the world, the lands of the Māori had been colonized. Yet, that was merely the beginning of the process, not the end.

Chapter 5 – Struggle for Identity and Sovereignty

From the perspective of the Māori chiefs, it seemed like the Treaty of Waitangi and the proclamation of British sovereignty wouldn't change the dynamics of relations with the Pākehā. Up until the 1840s, foreign immigration occurred on Māori terms, and the relationship with the European settlers was, for the most part, mutually beneficial. Yet all that was to change quickly.

Indeed, in the immediate aftermath of the Treaty of Waitangi, not much changed. Despite all the pompousness, Hobson's newly founded government had no actual power. It was poorly funded, numbering some fifty officials, representatives, and lawmen. In fact, the British government still relied upon Māori consent and goodwill. Despite that, Hobson transferred the capital of the newly founded colony from the Bay of Islands to Auckland in February 1841. This was coupled with a royal charter that finally established New Zealand as a separate crown colony, one independent from New South Wales. The charter was signed by the queen in November of 1840, and it came into effect in May 1841. With that, Hobson officially became the governor. Yet, even so, his government still relied on the Māori, especially since the Crown intended the colony to be funded by reselling the Māori land.

With that in mind, the Māori chiefs most likely expected a continuation of similar relations as before, with them dictating the terms to the Europeans. What they couldn't have imagined was the sheer numbers of the Pākehā who were yet to come. In previous decades, most of the Māori never actually had a chance to have direct contact with the Europeans. There were maybe up to three hundred foreign settlers in the 1830s, while their number rose to some two thousand in 1840. However, as the word began to spread about a new land of opportunities in the east, immigration began to speed up. The Europeans started coming in the thousands. This was only furthered in the following decade when the New Zealand government worked hard to entice new arrivals. By the late 1850s, the Pākehā outnumbered the Māori, with their numbers being roughly 59,000 to 56,000, respectively. Such numbers must have been unimaginable to the chiefs signing the treaty less than two decades before.

With the increased number of Europeans came diseases from the "Old World." While these were present in previous periods, the relatively small immigrant population meant those diseases were localized and rarely spread far. With increased interaction, influenza and measles spread among the Māori, who, despite decades-long contact with the Westerners, hadn't formed basic immunity to these. Combined with their already rough and unhygienic living conditions, many began to suffer. Even worse, the diseases began to circulate among all of the tribes, even those in the interior that had little to no direct contact with the Pākehā. Because of that, the Māori population started to decline significantly. By 1858, roughly ninety years after the arrival of Cook, the number of Māori people had dropped to half of its pre-European population.

In addition to the European diseases, the Māori began to face increased cultural pressure from the growing number of Pākehā. The immigration to New Zealand was no longer controlled by the natives but by the foreigners. The most exposed tribes, those closest to major migrant settlements and ports, began to realize their identities, customs, and traditions might be swallowed up by the sheer number of Westerners. Even worse, the Pākehā began to encroach on the Māori lands. Some of that was simply a byproduct of misunderstanding over what ownership meant to the Māori. The Europeans never fully grasped that, for them, ownership was defined by several factors, like inheritance rights, the right of occupation and use, and the right of conquest. Another problem was that for the Māori, not using acquired land was the same as relinquishing ownership. Furthermore, their lands were communal, not personally owned. Thus, rightfully acquiring Māori land wasn't as simple as signing a deed. It required more effort, something most Pākehā weren't willing to do.

To make matters worse, some of them reverted to tricks and deceit to get Māori territory. For example, they dealt only with a fragment of the owners, ignoring parts of the tribe that were against selling, or giving fewer goods than the lands were worth or agreed upon. In some cases, the fraudulent traders even forged deeds and other documents. On the other hand, the Māori refused to recognize such trickery, sometimes using violence to deal with the deceitful Pākehā. The first serious clash after the Treaty of Waitangi came in mid-1843 when representatives of the New Zealand Company, a business based in the United Kingdom focused on systematic colonization, tried to expulse the Māori from the land they supposedly bought. Fighting broke out in Wairau Valley, near the modern-day city of Nelson, resulting in the deaths of some thirty Europeans and six Māori. Subsequently, Robert FitzRoy, Hobson's successor as governor, ruled that the so-called Wairau Affray was the settlers' fault. It seemed the colonists were trying to enforce what looked like a fraudulent deed to the land.

While the ruling suggests the government tried to deal with the issues rightfully, it should be noted that FitzRoy knew that the Māori still outnumbered the colonists and that they had enough arms to massacre them if provoked. The New Zealand government was still too weak to subdue them. Thus, the colonial government didn't rectify its relations with the Ngāti Toa *iwi* and its chiefs: Te Rauparaha and his nephew, Te Rangihaeata. In the aftermath of the Wairau confrontation, these two moved to their tribal lands north of the Cook Strait near Wellington to create a new stronghold. There, they were involved in new land disputes around the Hutt Valley. Disputes once again escalated into conflicts in the summer of 1846, in which Te Rangihaeata withstood the pressure of the British colonial army but eventually withdrew after other Māori tribes supported the government. At the same time, Te Rauparaha was arrested and held for two years without a trial, even though he didn't directly participate in the clashes. In the end, both chiefs lost their influence and power.

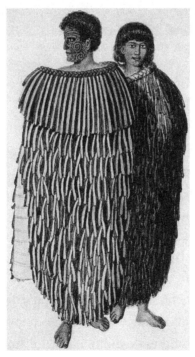

An illustration of Hōne Heke and his wife from the 1840s
Source: *https://commons.wikimedia.org/wiki/File:HoneHeke1845.jpg*

Painting of Heke cutting down the flagstaff from 1908 .
Source: https://commons.wikimedia.org/wiki/File:HekeFlagstaff.jpg

However, both of these conflicts were, in reality, still minor altercations, in which the Māori merely resisted the treachery of the European traders and settlers. A more important struggle erupted in the northern part of *Te Ika-a-Māui*, around the former New Zealand capital of Kororāreka (modern-day Russell) and the Bay of Islands. By 1844, Hōne Heke, a chief from the Ngāpuhi *iwi*, became disenchanted with the British rule, despite being the first signatory of the Treaty of Waitangi. It seems his personal grievances were with the fact that the new British government relocated the capital and imposed taxes, significantly lowering his income. However, there was also a strong sentiment against the Pākehā rule. For Heke, these feelings developed after the trial and execution of Wiremu Kīngi Maketū, the son of another Ngāpuhi chief, for murdering a European settler. For him, that was a clear infringement of the promised sovereignty in the treaty he signed. Other Māori shared similar views, seeing the treaty as just yet another Pākehā trick, with their ultimate goal being to seize all of the Māori lands.

The first signs of trouble came in mid-1844 when Heke's men cut down the flagstaff in Kororāreka, which was ironically Heke's gift to the district. It was a provocation and a message against British governance. However, no immediate response came, and the pole was rebuilt. In January of 1845, Heke cut down the flagstaff two more times, despite the guards surrounding it. By then, he had received support from Te Ruki Kawiti, another signatory of the treaty. Nevertheless, there were a number of other chiefs who remained loyal to the British, most notably Tāmati Wāka Nene. He even tried to reconcile Heke with the governor, acting as a mediator. Thus, when Heke and Kawiti attacked Kororāreka in March of 1845, he saw it as a betrayal. The struggle at the former capital was, at least in military terms, inconclusive, as both sides had casualties and neither achieved total victory. Nevertheless, the rebellious Māori troops managed to cut the flagstaff a fourth time while also penetrating the town. The fighting was cut short when a powder magazine exploded, setting the entire town on fire. While the citizens were evacuated, both the Māori and the Pākehā plundered the burning remains.

That was the official beginning of the so-called Flagstaff War, also known as Hōne Heke's Rebellion or the Northern War. After the Battle of Kororāreka, Heke and Kawiti retreated to more isolated areas. They built new forts far away from the Māori economic and civilian bases, luring the British from them. Over the next several months, the British army and navy proved quite inept in their struggles against the Māori rebels. Most notably, they had no proper answer for the improved *pās*, which were built with rifle warfare in mind. Even the ships' cannons weren't enough to crack them open. In fact, the only real defeat inflicted upon Heke and his men came from Nene at an all-Māori battle at Te Ahuahu. In all the other clashes, Heke and Kawiti managed to hold off the imperial troops before withdrawing for tactical reasons. In the end, after some ten months of warfare, Heke and Kawiti asked Nene to mediate the peace, ending the war in January of 1846.

The British were willing to accept this, as the war was disrupting the still-fragile economy of New Zealand. Thus, many claim it ended as an imperial victory, especially earlier scholars. This conclusion comes from the fact that the British retained control over the Māori. However, the end and the effects of the Flagstaff War are far from being that simple. Heke and his troops were never really defeated, and they still had a sizable fighting force. The real reason behind suing for peace was his realization that the war was draining his assets, which were limited. More importantly, Heke and Kawiti became aware that the British Empire and, in turn, the colonial government had a vaster pool of resources and could drag the conflict on almost indefinitely. Also, one should keep in mind that the Māori campaigns were usually short. There was no real way for the rebels to win, especially without the wider support of other tribes.

Nevertheless, Heke and Kawiti achieved at least partially what they intended. From then on, the colonial government was more careful in dealing with the Ngāpuhi. They considered their opinions in matters of the northern regions of the North Island, around the Hokianga and the Bay of Islands. Furthermore, Heke's and Kawiti's mana and respect grew in the eyes of their peers, regardless of whether they agreed with their actions. In essence, they showed the colonial government that the Māori weren't taking the Treaty of Waitangi lightly. They held the governor and the British accountable. Thus, when taking a broader look at the conflict, both in military terms and goals, the result of the Flagstaff War can be most accurately summarized as a stalemate, with losses and gains on both sides. The only real political loser in the whole ordeal was FitzRoy, whose governance was cut short because of his perceived incompetence to oversee New Zealand. In late 1845, he was replaced by George Grey.

Picture of George Grey from the 1860s
Source: https://commons.wikimedia.org/wiki/File:GeorgeEdwardGrey01.jpg

Illustration of Heke, with his wife, and Kawiti from 1846.
Source: https://commons.wikimedia.org/wiki/File:HekeKawiti1846.jpg

The new governor proved to be crucial for establishing peace. Grey was considerate toward the Māori, upholding the Treaty of Waitangi to the best of his abilities. He curtailed the trickery of the Pākehā and respected the Māori understanding of ownership. He protected their lands for as long as they refused to sell them. Once they decided to relinquish their territories, the government acted as an intermediary, gaining additional profit by reselling it to the new settlers. Grey's ability to govern the Māori came from his understanding of their culture and customs, which he learned after mastering their language. Grey even gathered Māori traditions and legends, which were subsequently published both in Māori and English. Because of such dealings, even Heke and other rebellious chiefs accepted him in the role of governor. In return, Grey built hospitals and schools for the Māori, as well as subsidized some of their agricultural works, like mills. He also sent colonial magistrates to help spread justice and law across the lands. Of course, all of these actions weren't meant to only aid the Māori but also help them assimilate into the Pākehā civilization and expand New Zealand's economy in general. Grey was less successful with these goals as he always lacked the proper funding to achieve them.

Grey's ultimate achievement was the New Zealand Constitution Act of 1852, which he drafted. After it was passed by British Parliament, it allowed for the self-governing of the New Zealand colony. The act itself was mostly concerned with establishing New Zealand's General Assembly and the Executive Council, but it also divided the colony into provinces and prescribed forms of local government. It also left open the possibility of Māori districts, showcasing once again Grey's concern with matters of the native population. In those districts, Māori laws and customs were to be preserved as long as they were not repugnant to the general principles of humanity. The Māori were also to be given the right to govern themselves when it came to dealings among themselves in particular districts. Unfortunately, these districts never materialized, yet in theory, the Māori had the right to vote if they passed the requirements as any other citizens of the colony. However, the problem arose that one of the prerequisites was owning a certain amount of land, something that the communal nature of Māori ownership blocked. Regardless, the Māori of that period showed little interest in the settlers' parliament, making such an exclusion, whether it was intentional or not, less impactful.

Along the way, the Pākehā population continued to grow, exerting additional pressure both on the Māori and on the lands. Within a few decades, the Western settlers managed to cause a natural disaster on an unprecedented scale. The Māori extinction of the moa pales in comparison. By clearing and changing the landscape and introducing new animals and plants, the Pākehā managed to decimate native wildlife in all forms. Numerous indigenous birds, plants, and fish couldn't deal with the new competition. And like the Māori, they suffered from various diseases brought by new "exotic" species. Worst of all is that many of the imported wildlife was brought in to make the settlers feel more at home. In other cases, there were economic reasons. Most notable was the introduction of sheep, which by the 1850s became one of the main economic forces of the colony, as wool became its primary export. The *Te Waipounamu* sheepherders found natural pastures, while on the North Island, these had to be created by clearing forests. Apart from agriculture, the settlers also searched for gold and coal, which were found in later periods. A gold rush happened in the early 1860s, which, in turn, brought more people and pressure on New Zealand wildlife and the Māori people.

Despite that, after Heke's rebellion, the Māori-Pākehā relations remained peaceful and cooperative. The colonial government respected Māori land ownership, and an economic interdependency remained in place. The Western settlers, who lived largely on New Zealand's coasts, were still relying on the Māori in the hinterlands for various resources and products. This division was more pronounced on *Te Ika-a-Māui*. Yet, the spheres of the Māori and the Pākehā remained largely separated, as they interacted only sporadically and superficially. Despite the wishes of the colonial government, the Māori were far from being "civilized." Yet this relative balance was slowly crumbling. On the one hand, the settler numbers continuously rose, as more and more people sought their fortunes in New Zealand. On the other hand, the Māori population was dwindling, as they were still plagued by illnesses and an unhygienic lifestyle.

Both sides were aware of the changing balance, rekindling old issues. On the Māori side, there was an increased fear that their customs and culture would perish if the tribes didn't take some active steps to preserve them. Thus, in some areas, the Māori tribes began to hold out on selling their lands. However, the Europeans believed the Māori population decline would eventually deliver them the territories they desired. Some Māori chiefs saw withholding land only as a partial solution. In the 1850s, there was a growing sense of "Māoriness" among the various tribes, a notion of identity that transcended their *iwi* distinction. Furthermore, many believed that the main strength of the Pākehā was their unity, something the Māori clearly lacked. Thus, a number of northern tribes began holding councils, creating a unified front against the settlers. These meetings, which were largely led by Tāmihana Te Rauparaha, son of the Ngāti Toa chief Te Rauparaha, also bred the idea of tribes combining their mana into a single Māori king. This movement became known as the *Kīngitanga*, which initially culminated in crowning ailing Chief Te Wherowhero of the Waikato *iwi* as the Māori king in 1858.

Upon his coronation, Te Wherowhero took the name Pōtatau and attempted to mitigate colonial concerns by proclaiming that a Māori king was in accord with the English queen. It wasn't an attempt to regain independence; it was a move to unify the Māori tribes. Nevertheless, for the colonial government and the majority of the settlers, it was a clear sign of disloyalty. Even worse, it was a challenge to additional land acquisition, which concerned the rising number of immigrants.

The Pākehā wanted to teach the natives a lesson in humility. The perfect opportunity came in 1859, when Pokikake Te Teira, a minor chief of the Te Atiawa *iwi*, decided to sell some land in the Taranaki region, located on the southwestern tip of the North Island. However, its paramount chief, Wiremu Kīngi Te Rangitāke, opposed the sale, stating that Te Teira had the right to sell the lands. The colonial government ignored Kīngi's rightful plea and went through with the sale to punish the Māori and their *Kīngitanga* movement. However, after almost a decade and a half of peace, the Māori decided to defend their rights with arms. A small detachment of Kīngi's warriors entered the disputed land and was forcibly removed in early 1860, giving a rightful cause to the other Māori tribes and sparking the so-called Taranaki War.

Unlike the Flagstaff War, the colonial government seemed more prepared for this war. It summoned additional troops from Australia, which together with local garrisons and militia brought the imperial forces to about 3,500. Against them stood a Māori army that fluctuated from several hundred to 1,500 at its peak. On paper, the British army should have won easily, but once again, the Māori proved to be a much tougher nut to crack, especially their impregnable *pā*s. Early in the war, the imperial forces managed to "storm" several of these forts, but these usually turned out to be abandoned.

But in June, the colonial army finally attacked a manned *pā* known as Puketakauere, which turned out to be a major defeat. Despite having artillery pieces and the numerical advantage of some 350 soldiers against roughly 200 defenders, the Pākehā troops fell to a well-disguised Māori ambush. In the end, the defenders had no more than five casualties, while the British had sixty-four, almost one-fifth of their engaged troops. In the following weeks, the Māori strengthened their string of forts in the region known as *Te Arei* (the barrier), practically besieging the immigrant settlers in their principal settlement in Taranaki named New Plymouth.

Illustration of Pōtatau Te Wherowhero made in the 1840s Source: https://commons.wikimedia.org/wiki/File:P%C5%8Dtatau_Te_Wherowhero_by_George_Frence_nch_Angas.jpg

Later 19[9]*-century painting of Wiremu Kīngi Te Rangitāke. Source: https://commons.wikimedia.org/wiki/File:Wiremu_Kingi,_by_Gottfried_Lindauer.jpg*

The tides of war began to shift in September when part of the Māori returned to their homes to help with planting the crops. This was followed by a slow and cautious imperial campaign aimed at weakening *Te Arei* and building a series of redoubts to counter them. However, the advance was sluggish, and the continuous war began to pile up the costs. Even after achieving several smaller victories and the destruction of a number of *pās*, the colonial command expressed doubts that further campaigns would seriously wear down the Māori.

Finally, in March of 1861, both sides agreed to a truce in which neither side actually agreed on much except to stop fighting. The end result of the war is once again mixed. The British failed to exert dominance over the Māori, while the Māori failed to regain control over the disputed lands. Furthermore, though the colonial army had slightly higher losses in crude numbers, the Māori lost more in percentage. Even worse for them, the Pākehā could afford to lose more people. Nevertheless, the military stalemate was at the time seen, somewhat rightfully, as a British failure and a Māori success.

However, it was a double-edged victory. While it provided a much-needed boost to the *Kīngitanga*, proving once again that the Māori could stand up for their rights, it also brought the movement more into the crosshairs. Seeing that the indigenous population was becoming increasingly rowdy, the British imperial government decided to return Grey to the post of New Zealand's governor, as he had been redeployed to South Africa in 1854.

However, his second term was significantly different than the first, as he showed no understanding of the *Kīngitanga* and Māori worries. Instead, upon his arrival in September of 1861, he began his plans to deal with insubordination. Grey tried to erode the Māori King Movement by implementing "peace policies," introducing a system of Māori local administration, and returning the disputed lands to the Te Atiawa tribe. He may have hoped this would defuse the situation, but it also helped appease tribes farther away from the *Kīngitanga* center, weakening the movement. At the same time, Grey continued with his "war policy," gathering troops and supplies and building infrastructure to enable him to strike at the heart of the Māori king.

In the end, it turned out that Grey, despite his genuine care for the Māori during his first governorship, suffered from the inherent racism held by the British government. He still saw the Māori as half-savages whose survival required them to surrender and assimilate with the superior British civilization. Thus, it seemed that he merely waited for an opportunity to strike down the insubordinate Māori. The chance arrived in early 1863, for tensions once again rose in the Taranaki region around the disputed land. Days before Grey proclaimed its return to the Te Atiawa *iwi*, a Māori party ambushed colonial forces as retribution for being ousted from one of their strongholds in the prior weeks. This caused low-intensity clashes between small Māori war parties and local garrisons, starting the so-called Second Taranaki War in May of 1863, even though it was, in essence, a mere continuation of the original conflict.

In their efforts to restore order, the colonial government sent reinforcements to Taranaki, slightly escalating the fighting in early June. However, this conflict was merely used as a pretext for Grey's actions against the *Kīngitanga*, which was centered in the Waikato region, west of the Bay of Plenty. On July 9th, he issued an ultimatum to the Māori in the region: Pledge an oath to the queen or suffer the consequences. Many able-bodied Māori took their weapons and went into the jungle, realizing there was trouble brewing. Two days later, Grey issued a proclamation, charging the *Kīngitanga* leaders with instigating unrest in Taranaki and plotting against the peace in New Zealand. This was followed by the final ultimatum—lay down arms, or face war. Without waiting for any response to this proclamation, Grey ordered an attack on Waikato Māori, which was ostensibly a preemptive assault to thwart their planned attack on Auckland. In July of 1863, the invasion of the Waikato began, the largest and often deemed the most significant campaign of all New Zealand Wars.

The initial colonial force numbered "only" four thousand well-prepared soldiers, who attacked new and unfinished entrenchments at Koheroa. The lightly guarded post was easily overrun, but the Māori threatened imperial supply lines with ambush attacks. Thus, initially, the government troops advanced slowly, building redoubts along their supply routes and waiting for reinforcements. Against them stood a line of Māori *pās* around the Waikato River. To aid with the advance were new troops and two riverboats armed with twelve-pounder guns. Throughout the southern winter, the fighting remained on a small scale and sporadic. Yet, by October, the British force grew up to eight thousand men in total, and it began its push into the Waikato region. The Pākehā troops moved up the Waikato River, following their flotilla. They forced the *Kīngitanga* forces to retreat to their second line of defense. Finally, in late November, the first major battle occurred at the Rangiriri *pā*, where some 1,400 colonial soldiers, backed with gunboats, overcame some 500 Māori defenders, opening up the rest of the Waikato Basin to the British advance.

A contemporary sketch of the battle at the Rangiriri pā. Source:
https://commons.wikimedia.org/wiki/File:The_repulse_of_the_royal_navy_storming_party_ra
ngiriri_pa.jpg

By early December, the colonial army entered Ngāruawāhia, the capital of the *Kīngitanga*. The Māori retreated farther south, building the strongest defensive line of the war. Their several large forts, centered around Paterangi, which was the largest of them, were built to block the main approaches to the agriculturally rich Rangiaowhia district. However, in February 1864, the British forces bypassed them and attacked the civilian population. What ensued was a massacre, as the Pākehā troops terrorized the elderly, women, and children in Rangiaowhia. They killed civilians, burning some alive in their homes, and raped women in front of the children. Not even the sanctuary of church or surrender was observed. This, in turn, forced the abandonment of the Paterangi line, as it was no longer viable for defense. What survived of the *Kīngitanga* army and supplies withdrew once again, taking a new stand at Ōrākau. There, the collective Māori leadership made an error by not listening to their most capable general, Rewi Maniapoto, a Ngāti Maniapoto chief. Rewi wanted to find a better location, but the joint leadership was adamant. On March 31ˢᵗ, the colonial troops encircled them, leading to a three-day-long battle that ended with a Māori further withdrawal. It became the bloodiest Māori loss of the war, with some 160 casualties.

After Ōrākau, the Pākehā forces switched their focus on the Tauranga region, specifically on the western shores of the Bay of Plenty. It was a ploy to cut off supplies to the Waikato Basin, as it became obvious that a single decisive victory would not come. The Māori forces proved too adept in retreating from their forts. In Tauranga, the colonial troops suffered a somewhat shameful defeat at Gate Pā, where the breaching British soldiers were routed by a Māori ambush. Following that, the Māori warriors retreated, but in June 1865, the Tauranga resistance was crushed in the Battle of Te Ranga when the imperial army stormed an unfinished fort. With that, the invasion of the Waikato was factually over, even though no armistice was agreed upon. It should be noted that in some cases,

Waikato and Tauranga are seen as separate campaigns. In any case, after suffering the morale-breaking string of defeats, the *Kīngitanga* movement, now headed by King Tāwhiao, Pōtatau's son, retreated farther into the hinterland in the west of the North Island. Henceforth, that region became known as the King Country or *Te Rohe Pōtae*, the name it still holds.

The invasion of the Waikato, as Grey planned, turned out to be a showpiece of British superiority. Despite the *Kīngitanga* movement's valiant struggle, it was no match for the colonial army. First of all, its troops most likely never peaked over four thousand men, while in previous campaigns, its numbers fluctuated. Despite its name, the movement never really reached political unity, and it still functioned more like the tribal alliances of the olden days, providing unreliable numbers of troops and collective leadership. Furthermore, the Māori warriors were still, for the most part, tied to the land, meaning they had to tend to their fields or their families might risk starvation. With that in mind, it is clear they stood little chance against the colonial force, which peaked at around fourteen thousand men, most of whom were professional soldiers brought by Grey to pacify the Māori. Furthermore, they had more resources and better weapons, including artillery. Yet, even with that supremacy, the Pākehā didn't manage to strike a deathblow to the *Kīngitanga* and the Māori spirit.

Nevertheless, the Waikato campaign proved to be a crucial step in defining future relations between the Pākehā and the Māori, allowing Grey to finally punish the brazen resistance to the Crown. The relationship between the two spheres of New Zealand was no longer mutually beneficial nor as cordial as before.

Chapter 6 – Rising up from the Bottom

The defeat of the *Kīngitanga* in Waikato was a devastating blow to the morale of the Māori, who started to feel more and more inadequate when it came to facing down the Europeans. The struggle also cost them some one thousand casualties, a considerable loss considering that the entire Māori population on both islands was just over fifty thousand. However, the worst for the Waikato tribes was Grey's land confiscations.

After achieving a significant, though not definite victory, over the "disloyal" Māori, the colonial government was determined to strike two birds with one stone. Grey ordered the confiscation of some 480,000 hectares (roughly 1,900 square miles) of Waikato land. This could have been seen as a "just punishment" if the seized land had been taken according to the tribes' participation in the war. However, the colonial government took only the most fertile and strategically important territories. Thus, some *iwi* and *hapū* lost their lands despite remaining completely loyal to the Pākehā, and others who ferociously fought against them remained largely unscathed. This suggests that, in the end, the entire war was fought over land, not loyalty or sovereignty. Furthermore, it suggests that for the Europeans, even

Grey, who got to know the Māori deeper than most other officials, all the Māori were the same. Another important point is that this confiscation was legalized by the New Zealand Settlements Act of 1863. The act allowed the seizure of land from Māori tribes that had rebelled against the colonial government after January 1st, 1863. This also allowed Grey and his staff to confiscate territories in other regions, most notably in Taranaki, which was at the time still engulfed in low-intensity conflicts.

The severity of the Second Taranaki War increased in early 1864. This was caused by the rise of the Pai Mārire movement, also known as Hauhau. It was a syncretic religion that incorporated biblical and Māori spiritual elements. It promised its followers deliverance from Pākehā domination. Though it was, in essence, peaceful—its name meant "Good and Peaceful"—the Pai Mārire followers used it to fuel their struggle against the colonial government. By April, the Taranaki Māori, reinvigorated by the new faith, assaulted some of the Pākehā strongholds but were defeated. Rekindling the conflict prompted Grey to relocate more troops to the region. By early 1865, almost four thousand additional soldiers had been deployed. They were ordered to secure "sufficient possession" of the lands the government had confiscated. The campaign was slow, encumbered by rough terrain and supply issues, but the colonial army continued to inflict defeats on the local tribes. Yet, even so, the Taranaki Māori continued to resist, prompting a shift in the Pākehā strategy.

By late 1865 and early 1866, they reverted to terror tactics. Colonial troops began attacking and destroying villages, killing the inhabitants and destroying homes and crops. This was then followed by looting. These attacks were indiscriminate of loyalty, as their goal was to inflict the utmost punishment on the enemy. The ferocity was such that even some of the British soldiers and civilians voiced their disapproval. Nevertheless, the Taranaki Māori began to fear further conflict. This was accompanied by the destruction of their forts and the building of British redoubts, which shifted the balance of power utterly in the colonials' favor. Seeing there was no sense in continuing the struggle, the Taranaki tribes finally laid down their weapons in September 1866. However, the ensuing peace was far from cordial, as it was followed by more confiscations and an influx of Pākehā settlers.

While the Taranaki Māori fought their battles, Pai Mārire spread among some of the tribes on the eastern coast, between Hawke's Bay and Poverty Bay. These eastern converts were led by Kereopa Te Rau, whose family was massacred in Rangiaowhia, leading him to blame much of the annihilation of innocent civilians on the missionaries' complicity. As a symbol of his resentment, in March of 1865, he executed a German Lutheran missionary, sparking outrage from other Christian Māori tribes. They sent out their war parties to hunt down Pai Mārire converts, starting the so-called East Cape War. Unlike other conflicts, where Māori fought mainly against the colonial forces, this was more akin to a Māori civil war. However, the loyal Māori, often labeled as *kūpapa* or collaborator, provided the bulk of the fighting forces, and they were supported by the Pākehā troops, which were trying to reestablish peace. The intensity of the fighting varied, reaching a peak in November of 1865. By late 1866, most of the Pai Mārire followers had been subdued. Some were killed, some scattered, while others were imprisoned and sent to the Chatham Islands.

Photograph of King Tāwhiao from the 1890s
Source: *https://commons.wikimedia.org/wiki/File:TawhiaoNLA.jpg*

Illustration of Te Kooti from the 1870s
Source: *https://commons.wikimedia.org/wiki/File:TeKootiCalvert.jpg*

Among the prisoners was Te Kooti Arikirangi Te Turuki, a Pai Mārire follower and self-proclaimed prophet. After two years of exile, Te Kooti managed to escape and returned to *Te Ika-a-Māui*. Upon landing at Poverty Bay with some two hundred followers, he asked for a pardon but was refused. Seeing there was no other way, Te Kooti resorted to violence, starting a series of raids against the Pākehā and kūpapa Māori while constantly evading his pursuers, which were a mix of colonial and Māori warriors. While it later seemed that pardoning him and his followers would have been much easier, in mid-1868, a new conflict was also erupting in Taranaki, prompting fear that Te Kooti's presence could be a trigger for a new war on the eastern coast. However, by underestimating him, the colonials had to face two simultaneous confrontations.

The Third Taranaki War, more commonly known as Tītokowaru's War, began in June of 1868 when the Taranaki Māori once again rebelled against the confiscation of their lands and the further immigration of new Pākehā settlers. The conflict was led by Riwha Tītokowaru, another Pai Mārire prophet, who mobilized a small but rather fanatical force behind him. Like Te Kooti, he, too, proved to be a capable general, managing to snag several victories against the more numerous colonial forces. In early September, the Taranaki Māori managed to impose a shameful defeat on the colonial forces while defending his *pā* at Te Ngutu o Te Manu. Tītokowaru's experience from previous wars served him greatly, yet his movement never managed to grow, leaving his fighting force at merely some two hundred warriors. Nevertheless, the colonial government realized that if he managed to gather enough traction among the wider Māori population, he would pose a serious threat. Some 1,250 Pākehā and Taranaki kūpapa Māori refocused from Te Kooti to Tītokowaru and began hunting him, but they were once again soundly defeated in November. It seemed that Taranaki would be left to Tītokowaru's mercy, as the demoralized colonial army once again switched its focus on Te Kooti in the east, hoping to liberate the eastern forces to deal with Tītokowaru.

After failing to deal with the eastern rebellion, the colonial forces returned to Taranaki in January of 1869. They began preparing for another showdown with Tītokowaru but never received one. In February, Tītokowaru's force suddenly disbanded, leaving only an empty *pā* at his new center at Tauranga-ika. There was no explanation for this abrupt ending, though some scholars have speculated that Tītokowaru made some sacred transgression, leaving him without further support. In any case, Tītokowaru was pursued, but he was never caught. This marked the end of the open struggle in the Taranaki region, leaving it under the mercy of the colonial government. Despite that, Te Kooti was still causing trouble on the eastern coast. Several attempts to capture or defeat him failed, and he and his followers retreated into the woods. The colonial government brought reinforcements from Taranaki to the east, but Te Kooti once again managed to evade his pursuers, raiding the Māori tribes that refused to shelter him. By July, he had retreated to the King Country, hoping to gain an alliance with the *Kīngitanga*.

A lithograph from the 1890s depicting a Māori ambush during Tītokowaru's War. Source: https://commons.wikimedia.org/wiki/File:Von_Tempsky%27s_death_Kennett_Watkins.jpg

This was troublesome news for the colonial forces, as they feared it might rekindle broader conflicts. However, it seems Tāwhiao held little respect for Te Kooti, and the majority of the *Kīngitanga* leaders were opposed to more hostilities. In the end, Te Kooti was given only shelter and supplies. The only military assistance came from Rewi Maniapoto. That only lasted until September, as Rewi became unimpressed by Te Kooti's defeat against a kūpapa fighting force. Thus, Te Kooti remained alone, and he attempted several more failed attacks in late 1869. From then on, he was on the run, evading the government forces, which were by then almost exclusively made up of kūpapa Māori. The pursuit lasted for roughly two more years, but in that time, Te Kooti's War became merely a series of smaller skirmishes and supply raids. Finally, in early 1872, Te Kooti realized he had no other option but to abandon his cause. In May of that year, he once again asked for sanctuary from the *Kīngitanga*, which he was given. That ended the last armed struggles of the Māori against the Pākehā, ending the conflicts collectively called the New Zealand Wars.

The result of these conflicts proved to be devastating on several levels. Firstly, it demoralized a large number of the Māori. This string of defeats was seen as a loss of mana and brought about a heightened feeling of inadequacy in comparison with the Europeans. Even worse was the cumulative loss of lands. Through various confiscations legalized by the New Zealand Settlements Act, as well as other laws like the Public Works Act of 1864, which allowed Māori land to be taken for public works, the North Island tribes lost somewhere between 1.2 and 1.3 million hectares (around 5,000 square miles) of their land. In perspective, *Te Ika-a-Māui* in total has some 11.4 hectares (44,000 square miles). To make matters worse, the confiscated lands were the most fertile. Not only did this prohibit them from trading with the Pākehā, but it also left many facing hunger and poverty. The fighting, famine, poor hygiene, and diseases brought the Māori population down to some 47,000 people in 1874, while the

Europeans were nearing 300,000. Thus, by the 1870s, most of the Pākehā, as well as some of the Māori, felt that it was only a matter of time before the indigenous people of New Zealand perished.

Looking at how the Māori life evolved throughout the second half of the 19th century contributed to such dim predictions. In general, it seemed that the Māori were on their way to adopting at least some aspects of the Pākehā culture. For example, most of them wore European clothes and adopted some form of Christianity. The Māori also built their homes with Western tools, materials, and styles in mind. However, some major technological improvements, such as the telegraph and railways, bypassed most Māori communities. On top of that, this supposed cultural demise could be described as a moral downfall. Alcoholism became a rampant issue among many tribes, as the Māori tried to find some escape from the grief that surrounded them. According to some testimonies, many Māori felt lost. They had no sense of direction in life and lived in despondency due to the many wars, Pākehā encroachment, poverty, and the continued suffering and death from illnesses.

Of course, alcoholism only worsened their health problems, which were caused by a lack of access to the health system and poor living conditions. In most cases, their homes remained crowded without proper ventilation or proper toilet facilities. They were perfect breeding grounds for diseases, and they easily spread since the Māori still lived communally. On the other hand, when they got sick, most European doctors and hospitals refused to treat them. Thus, in many cases, they turned to their traditional practices, which often made their condition worse. For example, they would purify influenza patients in water, which often led to pneumonia. Because of this, the Māori population continued to dwindle, falling down to forty-two thousand people in the early 1890s. By then, the number of Pākehā rose above 700,000, further confirming that the Māori were on the road to extinction.

This was, intentionally or not, helped by the fact that the Pākehā and Māori still lived in largely separated worlds. Over 90 percent of the latter lived in rural and often remote areas, which meant their plights were often disregarded by the colonial government. Thus, while the Pākehā benefited from government actions and investments, the Māori were left to fend for themselves. Apart from some governmentally funded schools, they got little from the New Zealand administration. However, this could also be seen as a double-edged sword, as it allowed the Māori to retain some of their hallmark traditions and language. Thus, while the majority accepted the core tenets of Christianity, they still retained the basic principles and ideas behind mana, *utu*, or *tapu*. Similarly, they continued to adorn their traditional clothes, mostly cloaks, when performing some of their traditional ceremonies. The Māori also preserved their basic social matrix, which revolved around the extended family unit. They often lived in one place alongside their tribal identities and connections. They also preserved their communal practices, which revolved around various assemblies and gatherings where all members could voice their opinions.

Furthermore, the Māori never stopped learning and adapting to new conditions. Like their ancestors, they were still able to notice which parts of Pākehā technology would benefit them. Because of that, they adopted various tools and European-style housing. It wasn't so much an attempt to culturally assimilate as much as it was reaping the benefits. This became especially important when the tribal leaders linked these improvements to better hygiene and a decrease in diseases. Relying on such adaptive practices ensured some gradual improvement in the Māori lifestyle as the 19th century came to an end.

Other aspects of Māori life also showed some signs of improvement. In 1867, Grey's government passed the Māori Representation Act, which introduced four mandatory Māori seats in the New Zealand assembly. These members were elected by Māori voters. All adult male Māori were allowed to vote. Thus, the Māori had universal male suffrage before the Pākehā. While this was done to appease some of the Māori, most notably the kūpapa, the New Zealand Wars still raged on. However, it introduced them to the political life of New Zealand.

Nevertheless, this meant little to the Māori. Most of their parliament representatives were from the loyal kūpapa, who mostly followed the government. An additional problem was that four seats weren't equal representation in terms of the percentage of New Zealand's population. At the time, it would have been more accurate for the Māori to have around fourteen to fifteen representatives. Even so, most of the Māori were still uninterested in "settler politics." Yet, minimal representation mattered; eventually, the idea of political participation blossomed among the tribes, and they began voting actively. This, in turn, allowed some of the non-kūpapa to sit in the assembly, where they voiced some of the Māori concerns.

Yet, the tribes still lacked the idea of national unity, despite the continued existence of the *Kīngitanga*. This meant that any political unity was almost unachievable. This fragmentation was helped by the fact that many tribes or even *hapū* of the same *iwi* had limited contact with other Māori. At the same time, the Europeans saw them all as a single entity, usually as "natives" without much local specificity. Nevertheless, this window into colonial politics provided the basis for later Māori voices to be heard.

Overall, at the turn of the 19th century, the Māori proved to be tougher than many had thought. They managed to preserve their cultural identity and language, and they also improved their quality of life. Some earned extra by working as laborers for the Pākehā, for example on farms or for lumber companies, while others managed to revitalize their local economies. This was followed by better housing, wider availability of basic education among the tribes, and better housing. Simultaneously, their representatives fought for some of their needs. All of this culminated in the gradual improvement of their lives, though they were still largely seen as second-class citizens and race by the Europeans. Nevertheless, due to these cumulative effects, the Māori population managed to grow and expand for the first time in over a century, reaching forty-five thousand in 1901. It was a sign that the Māori weren't ready to quit and that they were ready to transfer their struggle to survive from the battlefield to the political realm.

A photograph of a Māori village in the late 19ᵗ century.
Source: https://commons.wikimedia.org/wiki/File:Maori_Village.jpg

A clear sign of the change of the Māori struggle came as early as 1881 when the *Kīngitanga*, led by King Tāwhiao, officially laid down their arms and ended their exile. From then on, the political consciousness of the Māori grew, with many tribes fighting against unjustly seized lands through courts and other bureaucratic means. Along with that, more turned toward voting and politics, trying to better Māori lives through the actions in New Zealand's parliament. More importantly, in the last decade of the 19ᵗʰ century and in the early 20ᵗʰ century, some of the most prominent Māori leaders realized that their tribal divisions had to be overcome if they were to make a significant stand against the oppression they were facing. This led to more intertribal meetings and assemblies, which varied in their success and quality. But more importantly, it led to new pan-Māori organizations, like the Young Māori Party or the Rātana movement (*Te Haahi Rātana*). At the same time, the *Kīngitanga* finally started to obtain more than a local status.

All three of these groups acted on several levels and in different ways. The Young Māori Party, led by Māui Pōmare and Āpirana Ngata, focused on working with and within the colonial government to achieve gains in education, health, and the economy of the Māori. However, the Young Māori Party wasn't a political party but an association that worked on different fronts by individuals on their own accord. On the other hand, the Rātana was originally a religious movement founded by Tahupōtiki Wiremu Rātana, which then grew into its own church as well as a pan-*iwi* political movement. Its ideological goal was to unite the Māori people into a single group while also fighting on the political stage for their economic, social, and cultural betterment while still preserving their traditions. Finally, the *Kīngitanga* managed to transform into a pan-Māori movement thanks to Princess Te Puea Hērangi. She championed economic revival but without sacrificing Māori traditions. She also worked on reconciling with the Pākehā without compromising the Māori integrity and identity.

These political actions led to a significant turnaround in the Māori civilization. Their lands went through an economic revitalization, with new farms and other businesses being created or equipped with new technologies. The Māori were once again becoming an active part of New Zealand's economy, trading and dealing with the Pākehā and farther abroad. Literacy and education spread among the rural Māori regions without harming their language, crafts, and other traditions. Various Māori societies gained some access to medical care and knowledge, and thanks to intermarriage and closer connections with the Europeans, their population finally gained some immunity to the common Western diseases. Finally, it seems that, in general, hopelessness and depression were starting to vanish, as they no longer felt lost or destined to become extinct. All of these factors led to a rise in fertility, a fall in infant mortality, and a prolonged lifespan. Thus, their population grew to roughly sixty-seven thousand by the 1930s.

Despite all that, as well as the Pākehā boasting about having the "fairest" interracial relations, Māori life was far from equal or ideal. Most of them still lived in secluded and rural communities. Their income averaged lower than the Europeans, and they had a harder time receiving government aid and grants. Similarly, despite some advancements in health care availability, when the influenza pandemic, known better as the Spanish flu, hit New Zealand, it caused roughly four times more deaths among the Māori than the Pākehā. Considering that they made up around 4 percent of the total population, having 80 percent of the influenza-related deaths points to considerable deficiencies in access to medical care. Similarly, when the Great Depression hit New Zealand's economy in the early 1930s, the Māori made up an estimated 40 percent of the unemployed, and they also received lower benefits than the Pākehā. In general, racist prejudices were still alive, and they exhibited themselves more in times of crisis. Many felt it was better to lay off the Māori workers because they could "go back to the *pā* and get food and shelter." Despite all that, it is true that the government's treatment and general opinion of the Māori were improving, especially as more liberal and open-minded Pākehā politicians and generations came to power.

The Māori position among the Europeans was bettered for various reasons, mostly because of their hard work in achieving rights. However, another important factor was their participation in British overseas military actions. Initially, their wishes to join the South African War (1899–1902) were declined, as British policy was against using "native troops." Nevertheless, some Māori of mixed descent managed to join. With the First World War (1914–1918), this policy changed. The Crown accepted a contingent of five hundred Māori warriors in its service. By the end of the war, some 2,500 Māori served overseas, participating in many clashes, including the infamous Battle of Gallipoli. As such, they suffered significant casualties; more than three hundred were killed, and some seven hundred were wounded.

The war effort also showcased differences among the various Māori movements and tribes. Initially, the Māori contingent was filled with volunteers, but in 1916, conscription was introduced, as it was for the Pākehā. This was aimed especially at the Waikato tribes, who refused to join, as they still resented the loss of their lands in the New Zealand Wars. Similarly, the *Kīngitanga* movement opposed Māori participation, while the Young Māori Party urged their followers to join to prove they were peers to other men around the world. Many of the servicemen felt they had done just that and hoped that the equality with the Pākehā would continue when they got back home after the war. Yet, they were soon faced with disillusionment, as not much changed. Moreover, the Māori veterans didn't receive equal treatment and access to rehabilitation as the Pākehā soldiers. This pushed many of them toward the Rātana movement, asking for their equality.

Despite that, when the Second World War (1939-1945) began, the Māori began enlisting. Many were deployed in various infantry units, while some became pilots for the RAF (British Royal Air Force). However, at the start of the war, the New Zealand government agreed to form the 28th Māori Battalion, which was composed solely of Māori soldiers. Those who didn't serve in the army helped on the home front. This proved vital, as it started the urban migration of Māori. They went off to work in munition factories. The Māori communities also participated in fundraising.

By then, most Māori agreed they had to participate, but there were still some differences among them. For example, Āpirana Ngata wholeheartedly supported full Māori participation, hoping it would allow for further emancipation. On the other side stood the

Kīngitanga and Te Puea, who now advocated passive participation through the home front while also training to guard New Zealand from invasion. Yet, she was against warring overseas while the government still ignored their land grievances. Regardless of her messages, some 3,600 volunteers served in the Māori battalion. In total, just under sixteen thousand Māori soldiers were in the armed forces, serving in East Asia, the eastern Mediterranean, and Italy. The Māori battalion still had high casualties; they suffered over 2,600 casualties, with nearly 700 killed, which was 50 percent more than the average New Zealand units.

In the end, Ngata was proven right, though probably not to the degree he imagined. Many of the servicemen later entered the government and began working to better the Māori position in independent New Zealand. Simultaneously, by the early 1950s, most of the pre-war Māori leaders had died, leaving room for new generations to build upon their works. Yet more important than that was the fact that after the Second World War ended, New Zealand went through a period of economic prosperity and general optimism. Like most other nations, it also saw a population boom. Both of these facts proved crucial for the Māori. As the economy blossomed, it opened up more workplaces for them, especially in the realm of unskilled labor, which sped up the process of urban migration. Simultaneously, the Māori baby boom was significantly higher than the Pākehā, raising both their numbers and visibility. It also added an additional strain on tribal lands, which became inadequate to feed these growing numbers. This further contributed to urban migration, which, in turn, added to the Māori presence in New Zealand life. By the 1960s, the Māori constituted roughly 8 percent of New Zealand's population. Around 60 percent of them lived in urban areas, rising from the pre-war 11 percent.

Thanks to such developments, the Māori and the Pākehā once again began interacting on a larger scale, leading to confrontations of their views about themselves and the "other" group. The Europeans began revising their feelings toward the Māori and the unjustness of interracial relations. The Māori began revising their tribal identity. Thus, while there were some general improvements for the Māori, urbanization also brought a shock to their self-image. Many left their *hapū* and traditions to live in bigger cities, which were built around the Pākehā lifestyle. Willingly or not, they had to adjust, with some starting to lose their Māori identity, especially Māori children born in the cities. Since they were immersed in the Pākehā culture, they were largely cut off from their Māori roots. This led to feelings of being stuck in a cultural void, as they were neither full Māori nor really accepted by the Pākehā. This also endangered the Māori language and traditions since most of these weren't taught in schools. For a short while, it seemed that urbanization was the final step in assimilation and the subsequent disappearance of the Māori, especially since the government still saw it as the natural order of things.

However, by the late 1960s and especially in the 1970s, the Māori went through what was later dubbed a Māori renaissance. Thanks to a new generation of educated leaders who no longer held onto old notions of tribal and hereditary leadership, the fight for new sets of rights and equalities for the Māori people began. These included learning about their language and traditions in schools and laws that prohibited discrimination and created more equal opportunities, especially for higher education and better-paying jobs. This culminated with the Treaty of Waitangi Act of 1975 and the establishment of the Waitangi Tribunal, which, from the mid-1980s, began to reexamine previous expropriations and illegal acquisitions of tribal lands and the Pākehā-Māori legal relations in general. While the tribunal's actions were often criticized by both sides, its actions reinvigorated tribal activities, and reparations provided financial aid for many Māori families and tribes.

Of course, these changes weren't easy. They were followed by many protests and struggles since not all Europeans were ready to easily accept such developments. Yet these actions helped Māori culture and arts enter the mainstream, reinforcing the idea that they were an integral part of New Zealand, one that wasn't ready to disappear. Thus, from the 1980s onward, the position of the Māori changed significantly. They were no longer openly excluded and ignored by the Pākehā; they reached some level of social, economic, and cultural equality. In general, they lived lives that would have been unimaginable just a few generations before.

Thanks to all that, there are roughly 775,000 Māori in New Zealand today, which equates to roughly 16.5 percent (though it should be pointed out that in New Zealand, people can choose more than one ethnicity, meaning that combining all ethnic groups goes above 100 percent of the population). Of course, there is still room for improvement in many areas, and the Pākehā-Māori still aren't perfect with some of the inequalities that still have to be sorted out, but it seems that the future of the Māori is promising and bright. Most notably, they are no longer endangered.

Chapter 7 – Māori Civilization

Some aspects of the Māori culture and traditions were touched upon in previous chapters, like the all-permeating concept of mana. However, in most cases, these were brief descriptions, and many were generally excluded. While knowing more about the Māori culture might not be necessary to follow their story, it does add an additional layer of understanding and depth to their past. Thus, in this chapter, these aspects of the Māori, both past and present, will be expanded so you can get a fuller picture.

Before diving into this deep topic, a few clarifications should be made. Firstly, the Māori civilization in all its aspects has changed and developed a lot in the course of more than seven hundred years of their history. Secondly, like any other group, the Māori have their own regional differences and variations. With that in mind, creating an overarching and all-encompassing description of all the features and facets of the Māori civilization requires a book of its own. Thus, the descriptions in this chapter will be generalized and should be understood merely as broad brushstrokes of the Māori culture.

Another point that should be made is that the sources scholars use when dealing with these topics are varied and diverse. Some come from archaeological findings, while others are found in Māori oral traditions. Furthermore, some of the traditions often used are the written down versions made by the Europeans, usually in the 19th century. These are also aided and supplemented by early European accounts of the Māori culture. Furthermore, there are also some aspects of the Māori civilization that are being researched today among the modern Māori, such as their present understandings, recollections, and traditions. Finally, it is vital to remember that the Māori are still present, which means that their culture isn't something that is finalized. It is still evolving and developing like any other civilization.

With that in mind, the perfect place to start the story of the Māori civilization, a deeply spiritual and religious culture, is with their creation and foundation legends. Like most mythologies around the world, the Māori stories start with Te Kore (the void or chaos), which was followed by the emergence of Te Pō (the night) and Te Ao (the light). These divine concepts, represented as living beings, go through several stages of transformation; for example, Te Ao transforms into Te Aotūroa (the Long-Standing Light). It should be pointed out that in some versions, the creation and evolution of the universe is compared to a tree or a child in the womb. In any case, the nothingness of the universe was later filled by the creation of Ranginui (the Sky Father) and Papatūānuku (the Earth Mother), who lived in a tight embrace. The two of them had dozens of sons who lived in the confined darkness between them. These were the earliest gods or *atua*. They represented vital aspects of nature; for example, Tangaroa was the god of seas and lakes, and Tāne was the god of forests and birds.

Modern carvings depicting Ranginui and Papatūānuku in a tight embrace
Source: https://commons.wikimedia.org/wiki/File:WahineTane.jpg

Source: Carving by Bernard Makoare, Manos Nathan, and Lyonel Grant.Photograph by
Avenue., CC0, via Wikimedia Commons
https://commons.wikimedia.org/wiki/File:Carving_of_Tane_nui_a_Rangi,_at_Auckland_Zoo.jpg.

After some time, their children had had enough, and they decided to separate their parents. However, not all of the brothers were in favor of this. In most versions, Tāwhirimātea, the god of storms and winds, is the one against it, resulting in his anger at the other gods. He remains with his father, Ranginui, then proceeds to punish his brothers and their children with violent storms. Thus, the war among the god began. At the same time, he and his brothers fathered and created various new deities and supernatural beings. However, Tāwhirimātea proves to be better than most of the other gods, subduing and hurting Tāne and Tangaroa, as well as others like Rongo-mā-Tāne and Haumia-tiketike, the gods of cultivated and uncultivated plants. However, when he tried to deal with Tūmatauenga, the god of war, he failed, as Tūmatauenga embedded his feet in the earth. Eventually, Tāwhirimātea gave up, and peace was restored; however, storms and hurricanes still occasionally appear when his anger flares up.

Amidst all that, humankind appeared. There are several explanations for the creation of humans. Some are linked with Tāne, who either created the first female (Hine-ahu-one), the first male (Tiki), or both. Usually, their creation is connected with mud or dirt. However, there are some stories linking the creation of humankind to Tūmatauenga. Regardless, in the end, Tūmatauenga became more important to the humans. He got angry at the cowardice of his brothers and the fact they did not help him defeat Tāwhirimātea. He punished them, and through these punishments, Tūmatauenga invented the arts of hunting, agriculture, fishing, woodcutting, and cooking, showing the humans how to harness the resources of the natural world. Furthermore, the Māori learned about warfare through him.

From this point, there are several stories and myths explaining some other aspects of life and nature. Listing them all, especially considering all of the local variances, would be too much for this guide. Despite that, the brief retelling of the legend of Māui-tikitiki-a-

Taranga, known as Māui for short, is warranted considering its importance.

Māui is a Māori demigod and a hero who possessed superhuman strength and was capable of shapeshifting into animals. His achievements include slowing down the sun god, Tama-nui-te-rā, creating longer days for humans to finish their work in the process. He brought knowledge of how to tame fire, and he also created the first dog from his sister's husband. However, his most notable feat is catching a giant fish with an enchanted fishing line and magic hook, using his own blood as bait. Its body would become the North Island or *Te Ika-a-Māui*. Māui wanted to perform the appropriate ceremonies before cutting it up, but his brothers were impatient, causing it to crack and distort, creating lands and valleys instead of a great plain. From the same myth came the alternative name of the South Island, *Te Waka a Māui* or Māui's Canoe, as his *waka* supposedly became the landmass of the southern island. However, this myth is more common among the northern tribes, as the southern ones have a different legend centered around a mythical boy named Aoraki. Finally, Māui attempted to bring the humans immortality by tricking Hine-nui-te-pō, the goddess of the night and underworld. However, he failed. He became the first human to die, condemning all others to suffer the same fate.

These stories are clearly legends, an attempt to describe nature. As with other mythologies around the world, they aren't based on actual events. Yet, for the Māori, these stories were real and important, as they helped them to understand the world they lived in. The continuations of these legends are tribal traditions. These are the already mentioned stories about Kupe, Toi, the founding canoes, and their further dispersal across what would later be called *Aotearoa* by some Māori. These traditions are much more varied among the tribes, as they describe how a particular group came to a specific place. They also validate tribal territorial claims and the authority of *rangatira*, as well as explain alliances or friendly relations with neighbors. With that in mind, there is no particular generalization among them, and trying to do so could be seen as insulting to some of the *iwis*. What is important is to note that these stories are mostly human in nature and mostly located within New Zealand.

These myths and traditions were the core of what is often dubbed the Māori religion or *ngā karakia a te Māori* (literally Māori rituals). From them stemmed concepts of family and interconnectedness of the world, including humans and nature. In general, there was also a significant feeling of connection between the Māori and the land and its features, like lakes, rivers, and mountains. It should be pointed out that their mythology mentions a number of spirits or supernatural beings, and they are often connected with places and nature. There was also a belief in cyclicity due to the sun's movements, which also symbolized the cycle of birth and death. The Māori also liked the interrelation and the opposition of light and darkness (or day and night), with the former representing peace and understanding and the latter conflict and confusion. Because of those permeating beliefs of interdependence and connectivity among all things, living or not, the basis of the Māori religious beliefs were concepts such as mana, *utu*, or *tapu*, which guided those relations.

These concepts were incredibly important to the Māori, most notably mana, which signified an overreaching authority over everything, from people to the land. Its importance was so potent that it is often hard for non-Māori to comprehend it completely. However, the basis of all these ideas lies in other aspects of their beliefs. Firstly, there is *mauri*, the vital essence or energy that is present in most, if not all, physical objects in the world. Without it, mana couldn't flow into a person or an object. It is quite similar, possibly interchangeable, with the notion of *hau*, which also represents the essence or power of a being. In both cases, if the essence is lost, the person dies. Apart from the life force, there is also a notion of a *wairua*, the spirit that is separate from the body. Some of the Māori thought it resided in the heart or mind and that it lives on even after the death of a human being. *Wairua* can also briefly detach from the living body, for example in dreams, or give warnings and premonitions. The spirit is immortal; thus, connection with one's ancestors never ends.

Of course, all of the mentioned facets of the traditional Māori religion were conceptual, but like any other belief system, it also had practical parts. There was an abundance of rituals and ceremonies used to communicate with supernatural beings or manipulate energy and essence. The most complex and important ceremonies were carried out by *tohunga* (specialized experts), in this case, a priest or healer. The most basic rituals were chants or *karakia*, which relied on precise wording and structure, as well as the mana of the speaker. These chants covered a wide array of topics, such as to ward off bad luck, imbue weapons with strength, or weaken enemy war parties. There were also love charms and more serious *karakia* to raise or lower the mana or *tapu* of a person or place. These serious chants were usually part of more complex rituals that included various ceremonial acts. For example, *rāhui* was a ceremony that placed *tapu* on a particular place, while *whakanoa* removed it. *Whakahoro* would remove *tapu* from people. Important ceremonies followed the birth of a child, including dedication to a god and strengthening its mana and power. New buildings or canoes also had dedication ceremonies, while the *whāngai hau*, ceremonial food or offering, to an *atua* were also common.

Today, the most recognized and probably most misunderstood Māori ritual is *haka*, which is often associated with a war dance performed before a battle. While there were war *haka*, which were used to frighten the enemy and encourage one's own war party, *haka* covers a number of ceremonial dances. All of the *haka* have different movements and chants, and they are usually connected to a particular tribe. They can be performed as a welcome ceremony, a show of respect, funeral ceremonies, and much else. Likewise, they can vary from energetic and ferocious to calm and tame. They can be choreographed and organized or chaotic and more individualized.

The use of weapons or other paraphernalia was also diverse. Similarly, *haka* could be performed by various groups, including women and children, depending on the purpose and nature of the ceremony. Today, the use of *haka* across New Zealand is somewhat controversial, with the most famous example being New Zealand's rugby team performing *Ka Mate haka* before their matches. Depending on how it is used and portrayed, some Māori see it as cultural appropriation and disrespecting their traditions, while others may think of it as a celebration of their culture.

A Māori tribe performing the welcoming haka to a government official in 1904.
Source: https://commons.wikimedia.org/wiki/File:Haka_for_Lord_Ranfurly_1904.jpg

Of course, like with other cultural aspects, Māori mythology and religious rituals evolved as time passed, and they varied in specific details among the tribes. Thus, an important change occurred when Christianity arrived in New Zealand. As previously stated, by the turn of the 19th century, most Māori had officially converted to Christianity. However, in practice, many still held onto the Māori world views and notions. From these mixing religions came several syncretic religions, which usually revolved around a binding Christian God and Māori rituals and traditions. They also typically possessed a strong nationalist

Māori sentiment, and the followers struggled to preserve Māori identity against the European culture and faith. Another possible sign of Māori and Christian intermixing is the god Io Matua Kore. He was supposedly a supreme being, the creator of creators, who lived in Te Kore or the void. Yet, the issue of Io is a matter of great debate, as he was first mentioned in the early 20th century, and it is claimed to have been a "secret" belief held among the aristocracy and priests. Furthermore, Io is mentioned in other Polynesian mythologies but rather vaguely. Thus, some scholars claim it predates Christianity, while others see it as yet another byproduct of religious intermixing.

Regardless, Christianity won out against the traditional Māori religion. Today, only a few thousand Māori still identify as followers of their traditional faith. Tens of thousands practice some form of Māori Christianity, with more than half adhering to Rātana, which is followed by Ringatū (Te Kooti's faith) and Pai Mārire. Yet, even so, roughly 46 percent of Māori officially declare themselves as not religious today, a trend that is prevalent among other ethnicities of New Zealand. Over 50 percent of its population is either not religious or undeclared. Despite that, neither Christianity nor atheism fully replaced or extinguished Māori spirituality, which still plays an important part in their national identity. This isn't surprising, considering that Māori beliefs and religious notions permeated every other aspect of their culture and life.

These strong connections between faith and other facets of the Māori civilization are probably most easily recognized in *whakapapa* or genealogy. They form the basis of tribal identity, and the people pass these on to the following generations. Thus, *whakapapa* is a core part of mātauranga (Māori knowledge). Yet, at the same time, these oral traditions, which were memorized to the letter, can also be seen as a form of Māori literature, despite not being written down originally. Of course, there were different types of genealogies that traced various links between families and individuals, and each tribe had its own unique local tradition. *Whakapapa* was usually sung or recited, often to children, but they were also told as stories. *Tohunga* who specialized in genealogies were quite respected, and they often used sticks with notches or ridges to help them recollect all the lineages by having each ridge represent a specific ancestor. Another aspect of *whakapapa* was that it was built over the generations, forming a communal folklore tradition that spanned across time.

Carvings or *whakairo* were also an example of mixing art with religion. The Māori style evolved from general Polynesian carvings, quickly developing local specificities inspired by New Zealand's flora and fauna. Carvings usually represented gods, spirits, famous ancestors, or great chiefs. *Whakairo* could be made out of stone or wood, and they usually had decorative purposes. As such, they might be carved directly into walls, frames, or canoes, although it could also be a separate piece on its own. The carving was usually done by subtraction, with stylized forms that had different local variations that changed over time. For example, one of the styles was the serpentine (tuare) style, in which figures have cone-like heads and long, twisting bodies. Another example is the square style, which was exemplified by the broad, squatting-like posture of the body, with the head usually taking up about a third of the entire composition. Another important detail of most carvings was they were often painted with clay pigments. The religious part of the *whakairo* was that the Māori believed the carving would absorb the properties of the represented figures, meaning they could be *tapu* or imbued to become sacred. They were also used to expand and exhibit mana and the wealth of a tribe.

Similar importance lay with the Māori tattoos, which are today probably the most recognizable form of traditional Māori art. *Tā moko* had its roots in mythology, as a chief was supposedly taught the art of tattooing from the spirits of the underworld. Since producing quality tattoos required a lot of skills, the tattoo artists were often regarded as *tohunga*. The process itself was highly ritualized and considered *tapu*. While many Europeans linked *tā moko* with warrior feats, it was actually another way to showcase personal mana.

However, some people were so sacred that despite their immense mana, they couldn't get a tattoo, as piercing their skin would be seen as breaking their *tapu*. These could be highly important chiefs, persons of great lineage, or, more commonly, *tohunga* priests. Like other art forms, the details and styles of *tā moko* changed over time, and all tribes had some unique patterns of their own. The tools also changed, from bone and metal chisels to modern-day needles. Like other types of art, *tā moko* went through a resurgence in the 1960s, but it also seeped through to non-Māori, raising the question of cultural appropriation once again. While some Māori are against others using their traditional designs without any regard to their meaning or value, others see no problem in having tattoos inspired by their tradition as long as they don't call it *tā moko*.

Although their tattoos became rather intricate and of great importance, the Māori never developed much in the form of painted arts. While some of the oldest preserved artworks are painted cave walls from the Archaic period, it never became a pervasive art form. These early charcoal drawings were simple representations of various animals, humans, and supernatural beings. Yet, by the Classical period, the Māori used painting merely to decorate the wall panels of their homes. These paintings didn't receive much reverence as other types of visual arts, nor were the painters as celebrated as, for example, tattoo masters. Yet, all of those arts, including decorative paintings, used a spiral motif known as *koru* (loop or coil). It was based on the unfurling silver fern, which is native to New Zealand. It symbolizes peace, new life, growth, and strength while also conveying the idea of perpetual movement and the cycle of nature and life. In later periods, with the arrival of the Pākehā, the Māori adopted some of their figurative art styles and used less stylized depictions of nature and humans. New European paints also allowed for more colorful paintings. Despite that, Māori paintings didn't rise to prominence until the Māori renaissance in the late 20th century, when some contemporary artists began drawing upon their heritage to create new paintings.

Modern wharenui replica as an exhibit in a museum.
Source: 111 Emergency from New Zealand, CC BY 2.0
<https://creativecommons.org/licenses/by/2.0>, via Wikimedia Commons
https://commons.wikimedia.org/wiki/File:Wharenui_in_Te_Papa_museum.jpg

Māori architecture combined many aspects of Māori civilization. In general, their homes and buildings were simple huts; however, some more prominent structures stood out. *Wharepuni* (sleeping house), which often housed several families, were usually unadorned unless they belonged to a chief or some other prominent tribal member. A more decorated building was the *pātaka* (storehouse) since it represented tribal mana and wealth. Yet these paled in comparison to *whare whakairo* (literally "carved house"), sometimes also known as *wharenui* ("big house"), or *whare rūnanga* ("meeting house"). These buildings were communal centers with a single large room under a pitched roof, extending to an open porch. These buildings were elaborately adorned with carvings and paintings, combining abstract designs such as *koru* and the representations of gods and ancestors. This traditional form began to appear in the early 19th century, with some scholars arguing it was influenced by Christian churches.

Regardless, *whare whakairo* took a central place in Māori cultural and religious life. On the one hand, decorative images of ancestors in those buildings were personifications; thus, they were often regarded as living beings and embodiments of tribal identity and predecessors. Furthermore, the decorations were also helpful when teaching and reciting *whakapapa*, as parts of the building represented the most notable ancestors. The complexity of the structure's ornamentation and size exhibited tribal mana, and they also made it partly *tapu*. *Whare whakairo* was also intertwined with mythology, as well as a place where some rituals and ceremonies were carried out. As such, they became vital expressions of Māori identity, which, like many other facets, went through a decline and revival during the 20th century. While today the Māori use various architectural designs and styles, *whare whakairo* remains the most traditional and common for communal structures. Today, these buildings can be found anywhere where a large number of Māori are present, even if it's not strictly tribal related. An example would be schools or universities.

However, most *wharenui* are located within *marae* (often translated as an open area or a courtyard). Initially, *marae* was a place for communal practices, usually a simple clearing without any buildings. Yet as the *whare whakairo* spread, the two became interconnected as places for various rituals and traditions. Later on, these communal places were further expanded with new buildings, making it more akin to a complex than merely a courtyard. A common addition is a communal dining house known as *wharekai*. It usually had its own kitchen. The area is *tapu* and commonly a rectangular shape. It is marked with stones or wooden posts, and it is always located on communal land. *Marae* can belong to an *iwi* or a *hapū*, but in both cases, it represents a central place for some of the most important rituals. These include traditional Māori funerals (*tangihanga* or more commonly known as *tangi*), *pōwhiri* (welcome ceremonies), tribal debates and meetings, cleansing rituals, and a host of social and communal gatherings. The functionality and importance of *marae* are preserved to this day, and it plays a central role in many Māori communities.

The most practical gatherings held in *marae* were probably tribal meetings since the communal decisions made there would define the people's future. Nevertheless, *marae*, along with *whare whakairo*, played an important role in the arts. It was a place where public dances were performed, including various *haka*, and it was accompanied by Māori music or *pūoro*. These included various songs (*waiata*), such as love songs (*waiata aroha*) and laments (*waiata tangi*). Some of the earliest forms of songs were ancient chants (*mōteatea*). They repeated a single melodic line, usually centered around one note, falling away at the end of the last line.

These were sometimes accompanied by traditional instruments or *taonga pūoro*, including various flutes, trumpets, percussion, and twirling instruments. The music was part of the Māori mythology, which is evident by the fact that melody was associated with Ranginui and rhythm with Papatūānuku, while the instruments were linked with their *atua* or children. Music and chants were also integral parts of religious rituals, as they represented communication with the gods. As with anything related to religion, music was considered *tapu*, and it was used by priests. However, it was also used for entertainment but in a more private and less grandiose way.

Because of its importance, music and singing were parts of various ceremonies held in the *marae*. Today, the traditional instruments have mostly lost their spiritual meaning to the Māori, but their music can be heard at gatherings and in orchestral pieces and movies. On the other hand, the Māori also accepted other contemporary music genres and instruments.

Apart from rituals, *marae* was also a place where children were educated by various *tohunga*, passing on *Māoritanga* or Māori civilization and way of life to the next generation. This role is also maintained in modern times. Another practice was communal meals, which were sometimes prepared in *hāngī* or a pit oven. Today, *hāngī* is sometimes replicated with gas-powered metal ovens, and the ingredients used varied over time due to what was available. Nevertheless, it usually included both meat and vegetables. Additionally, *marae* was used for various celebrations and ceremonial events. Today, they also host birthdays, weddings, and anniversaries.

Apart from art and cultural events, *marae* was also home to Māori sports. Depending on the weather and type of event, these games were either indoors or outdoors. Most important were sports that prepared youth for battles, like *para whakawai*, also known as *whakahoro rākau*. It was basically a battle-sport, where participants exercised handling weapons, dodging, and parrying blows through sparring. The Māori also practiced wrestling, running, jumping, and throwing spears. Some of the less war-like sports were swimming, canoe racing, hide-and-seek, and playing on swings and see-saws. There were also less physical games that revolved around memory, words, and patterns. However, many of these were suppressed by the Pākehā missionaries, and many never fully recovered.

During the Māori renaissance, some were given new life, like, for example, canoeing. Others were partially recreated and changed to fit the new times. Today, the most popular Māori sport is *kī-o-rahi*, a ball game that shares some similarities with rugby. Teams score by touching the boundary markers or hitting a central target. While some scholars and Māori experts claim it is a traditional game, others say there is no firm evidence of how old it is. Apart from the traditional games, the modern Māori play a variety of European sports. They are probably most successful in rugby with New Zealand's "All Blacks" team. Finally, an important part of all *marae* events was the clothing worn. In everyday activities, the Māori traditionally wore little. Males sometimes wore only belts and strings that held their foreskins in place. Females wore short aprons over their pubic area. This began to change with the arrival of the Europeans, who saw it as an expression of their savagery. Thus, they imposed more clothing on them. The

Māori were willing to accept the Pākehā clothing, especially in the colder southern regions, as it provided more protection and warmth. Part of the reason the Māori wore so little was that the North Island climate was warm enough. In addition, weaving was a hard and time-consuming process, making clothing somewhat of a luxury. Traditionally, Māori made their clothing from flax, cabbage trees, and other native plants. These were used to weave ceremonial cloaks and kilt-like dresses. In some rare cases, dog skins and bird feathers were also used to adorn some of the more luxurious pieces. In most cases, these were dyed with color derived from various clays or tree bark.

Traditional simple rain cloak

Modern replicas of ceremonial clothing

Clothes were woven by hand, and the traditional *tāniko* technique, similar to twining, was used to create ornamental borders. These were most commonly found on cloaks, but they were also on decorative mats, as weaving was used for creating home decorations and household items. The most common designs consisted of triangles, diamonds, diagonal bars, and stepped patterns, mostly due to the limitation of traditional Māori weaving techniques.

Cloaks were divided into two broad groups. Most were practical robes that provided warmth and protection from the rain or wind, while the other was ceremonial. The latter was highly adorned; feathers, tassels, and even animal skins were used to decorate them. Dresses were usually worn for ceremonial proposes, and they were similarly adorned. Even the belts could be specially made for such purposes. However, even though European clothing became more dominant, these traditional clothing items remained in use in Māori rituals, even to this day. Apart from clothing, the Māori also used feathers and combs in their hair to further accessorize their looks. These, too, can be seen in modern recreations of traditional outfits. Yet, in general, the Māori fully accepted Western-style clothing in everyday life.

Finally, although the myth of the Māori being a nation of constant war and fighting has long been disproven, warfare was an integral part of their worldview and civilization. As with many other aspects of Māori life, war was interlinked with their religious beliefs. It was the central theme of their creation myth, and Tūmatauenga was seen as one of the most important deities. Thus, it wasn't uncommon for tribal conflicts to erupt because of cultural reasons. There were likely attempts to restore *utu* after an insult or trespassing, the breaking of some local *tapu*, or simply to restore or increase tribal or even personal mana. Of course, wars were also fought for more practical reasons, such as food and land.

The men fought in these conflicts, but women played an important role in ending them. One of the ways to ensure lasting peace was by arranging a marriage between the two groups, which was identified as "female peace." In contrast, peace made solely by men was seen as treacherous and troublesome. Apart from female peace, ritualistic peacemaking was also done by arranging the metaphorical "greenstone door" or *tatau pounamu*. In that case, the "door" represented safe passage, and greenstone indicated its longevity. In some cases, a *pounamu* was given to symbolize the end of a war.

As for the war itself, the weapons changed and evolved over time, but the basic Māori strategies revolved around trickery and ambush. However, rituals were integral parts of war as well. Firstly, priests blessed war parties before they went off to war, making its members *tapu*. Before a war, it was common to perform *haka peruperu* (a haka with weapons) to bolster morale and power. Achieving feats in combat was also a way to increase personal mana, with special prestige coming from making the first kill of the battle. After the battle was done, victors captured slaves, who were usually women and children. In some cases, members of the defeated party were slain, and parts of them, most commonly the heart, were eaten in a cannibalistic ritual. It signified both the ultimate humiliation as well as conquering the opponent's mana. However, cannibalism wasn't omnipresent, as it was a punishment performed only to one's worst enemies. Yet by the late 19th century, the practice had died out. Nevertheless, it also added to the European view of the Māori being brutal savages. Finally, after the war party returned home, the priests would lift *tapu*, and life would continue.

In terms of war prowess, the Māori proved their worth against the Pākehā, as well as in the two world wars. Yet, while their bravery and skill were valued, their *pās* were probably notorious in the eyes of the Europeans. Although these Māori fortresses had simple origins, they grew in size and complexity. Their palisades could be up to 5 feet (1.5 meters) tall and padded with bundles of flax to give additional protection against artillery fire. Palisades were often built in two lines, making them even more resistant to enemy bombardment. It was also common for them to have openings for gunmen to fire from trenches, and in some cases, structures were built over these trenches to add a second firing line above them. Tunnels and underground bunkers connected various parts of the fort, protecting the defenders from artillery fire.

The Māori *pās* were so well built that the British never found a reliable way of conquering them, even with their howitzers and mortars. Some scholars have even argued that dealing with the Māori forts influenced the British army, aiding in the development of trench warfare, which would become the hallmark of the First World War. Today, the Māori continue to serve in the New Zealand armed forces, using modern technologies and tactics. In the 1950s, they were fully integrated into the army, losing their separate battalion. The Māori soldiers fought in many wars, including the Korean War, the Vietnam

War, and the war in Afghanistan. While they still practice some of the Māori traditions linked with war, such as *haka* and ritualistic challenges to the enemy, warfare itself isn't as intertwined with religion as before. It became more of a way to prove Māori worthiness and value to the world.

This chapter gave a brief overview of some traditional aspects of Māori culture, though much more could be said in greater detail. In many regards, the Māori civilization revolved around religious beliefs, community, and family, as well as a strong sense of identity. It is also vital to note that, like the Māori people, their traditions didn't die with colonization. They adapted and survived, with many Māori practicing both their traditional arts and crafts as well as modern cultural expressions, such as films, popular music, books, and sports. They show no sign of giving up. They will persevere and pass *Māoritanga* on to new generations.

Conclusion

Looking at the story of the Māori people and stripping away decades of prejudices and overt racism, we see a colorful tale of adversity and adaptability to various troubles. The Māori, along with their Polynesian predecessors, managed to cross vast distances, learn about their new home, and create a unique and exceptional civilization, one rich with traditions and arts. They proved able to change and adjust to changing circumstances, surviving both times of long solitude and extended subjugation from the Pākehā settlers. Not only that, but they also managed to learn from their new neighbors, absorbing cultural and technological influences without surrendering their unique identity. Furthermore, they were ready to defend their civilization with weapons and politics. They refused to accept other people's evaluation that they were less worthy as a culture and people. In the end, they were able to find their rightful place among the nations of the world, standing just as tall and proud as any other.

Māori history, with all its ups and downs, was and still is a tale of stubbornness and identity. Looking at their history superficially, especially the clashes with the Western settlers and the adversities that came with them, it seems to have been a constant struggle, often bloody and filled with strife. Yet, it is also an example of learning how to coexist and learn from other people. The Māori and their past can teach us an important lesson, that working together often yields more benefits. At the same time, it also shows that it is not shameful to learn from others and accepting what is better without sacrificing personal identity or beliefs. Most importantly, the Māori showed the world that it's not important what others see in you but what you see in yourself. These lessons can be applied to whole nations, but they also apply to individuals as well. They show that history is the story of humankind as groups and individuals. History can always teach us how to better ourselves and expand our understanding of the world we live in.

Despite all that, this guide into the fascinating history of the Māori people is merely an introduction to their vibrant past and civilization. With any luck, it gave you a slightly broader and deeper picture of their history and culture, erasing preexisting stereotypies due to by decades of misrepresentation. More importantly, it hopefully inspired you to learn more about the tale of the Māori.

Here's another book by Captivating History that you might like

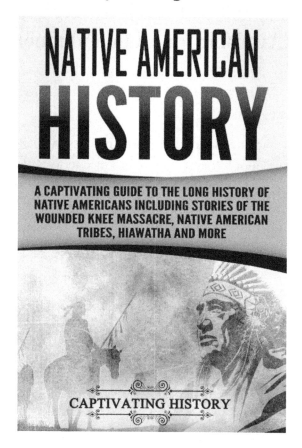

Free Bonus from Captivating History (Available for a Limited time)

Hi History Lovers!

Now you have a chance to join our exclusive history list so you can get your first history ebook for free as well as discounts and a potential to get more history books for free! Simply visit the link below to join.

Captivatinghistory.com/ebook

Also, make sure to follow us on Facebook, Twitter and Youtube by searching for Captivating History.

Bibliography

Alice Te Punga Somerville. *Once Were Pacific: Māori Connections to Oceania.* University of Minnesota Press, 2012.

Angela Ballara. *Taua: Musket Wars, 'Land Wars' or Tikanga?: Warfare in Maori Society in the Early Nineteenth Century,* Penguin Books, 2003.

Brendan Hokowhitu. "Haka: Colonized Physicality, Body-Logic, and Embodied Sovereignty." In *Performing Indigeneity: Global Histories and Contemporary Experiences,* edited by Laura R. Graham and H. Glenn Penny, 273–304. University of Nebraska Press, 2014.

Bruce McFadgen. *Hostile Shores: Catastrophic Events in Prehistoric New Zealand and Their Impact on Maori Coastal Communities.* Auckland University Press, 2007.

Christina A. Thompson (1997). *A Dangerous People Whose Only Occupation Is War: Maori and Pakeha in 19th-century New Zealand.* The Journal of Pacific History, 32:1, 109-119.

Danny Keenan. *New Zealand's Land Wars - A Māori Perspective.* Penguin Books, 2021.

Domenico F. Vaggioli. *The Maori: A History of the Earliest Inhabitants of New Zealand.* Edwin Mellen Press, 2010.

Geoffrey Irwin. *Kohika: The Archaeology of a Late Māori Lake Village in the Ngāti Awa Rohe, Bay of Plenty, New Zealand.* Auckland University Press, 2004.

George Grey. *Polynesian Mythology and Ancient Traditional History of the Maori as Told by Their Priests and Chiefs.* Taplinger Publishing, 1970.

Hirini Moko Mead. *Te Toi Whakairo: The Art of Maori Carving.* Libro International, 2016.

Ian Knight. *Maori Fortifications.* Osprey Publishing, 2009.

Ian Pool. *Te Iwi Maori -A New Zealand Population Past, Present & Projected.* Auckland University Press, 1991.

James Belich. *Making Peoples – A History of the New Zealanders from Polynesian Settlement to the End of Nineteenth Century.* Penguin Books, 1996.

James Belich. *The New Zealand Wars and the Victorian Interpretation of Racial Conflict.* Auckland University Press, 1986.

Jane McRae. *Māori Oral Tradition: He Kōrero nō te Ao Tawhito.* Auckland University Press, 2017.

Jørgen Prytz-Johansen. *The Maori and His Religion in Its Non-ritualistic Aspects.* HAU, 2012.

Keith Sinclair. *A History of New Zealand.* Penguin Books, 1991.

Keith Sinclair. *Kinds of Peace: Maori People after the Wars, 1870-85.* Auckland University Press, 1991.

Keith Sinclair. *The Origins of the Maori Wars.* Auckland University Press, 2013.

Leonard Bell. *Colonial Constructs: European Images of Maori 1840-1914.* Auckland University Press, 1992.

M. P. K. Sorrenson. *Ko te Whenua te Utu = Land Is the Price: Essays on Maori History, Land and Politics.* Auckland University Press, 2014.

M. P. K. Sorrenson. *Maori Origins and Migrations - The Genesis of Some Pakeha Myths and Legends.* Auckland University Press, 1979.

Mervyn McLean. *Traditional Songs of the Maori.* Auckland University Press, 2013.

Michael Belgrave. *Dancing with the King: The Rise and Fall of the King Country, 1864-1885.* Auckland University Press, 2017.

Michael King. *The Penguin History of New Zealand.* Penguin Books, 2003.

Paul Clark. *"HAUHAU" - The Pai Marire Search for Maori Identity.* Auckland University Press, 1975.

Pei Te Hurinui. *King Potatau: An Account of the Life of Potatau te Wherowhero the First Maori King.* Huia Publishers, 2013.

Philippa M. Smith. *A Concise History of New Zealand.* Cambridge University Press, 2012.

Poia Rewi. *Whaikōrero: The World of Māori Oratory.* Auckland University Press, 2010.

Raymond Firth. *Primitive Economics of the New Zealand Maori,* Routledge, 2011.

The New Zealand Geographic Board, *He Korero Pūrākau Mo Ngā Taunahanahatanga a Ngā Tūpuna / Place Names of the Ancestors - A Māori Oral History Atlas.* 1990.

Tom Brooking. *The History of New Zealand.* Greenwood Press, 2004.

Tony Ballantyne. *Entanglements of Empire – Missionaries, Māori and the Question of the Body.* Auckland University Press, 2015.

V. O'Malley, B. Stirling and W. Penetito. *The Treaty of Waitangi Companion: Māori and Pākehā from Tasman to Today.* Auckland University Press, 2010.

Vincent O'Malley. *The Meeting Place: Māori and Pākehā Encounters, 1642-1840.* Auckland University Press, 2012.

W. Ihimaera and W. Hereaka. *Pūrākau: Māori Myths Retold by Māori Writers.* Penguin Books, 2019.

Walter, R., Buckley, H., Jacomb, C., & Matisoo-Smith, E. (2017). *Mass Migration and the Polynesian Settlement of New Zealand.* Journal of World Prehistory, 30(4), 351–376.

William Edward Moneyhun. *The New New Zealand: The Maori and Pakeha Populations.* McFarland, 2019.

Made in the USA
Las Vegas, NV
13 May 2024

89894359R00075